Beyond Laravel

An Entrepreneur's Guide to Building Effective Software

by Michael Akopov

Written by
Michael Akopov

Managing Editor
Oscar Merida

Layout
Oscar Merida

Published by
musketeers.me, LLC.
4627 University Dr
Fairfax, VA 22030 USA

240-348-5PHP (240-348-5747)
info@phparch.com
www.phparch.com

Table of Contents

Dedication

*To my Dad, for teaching me everything I know
and for always being a stable voice in my life.*

Thank You

There is no shortage of people to thank and not enough words to express gratitude with. But I would be remiss if I didn't say a special thank you to my wife, my daughters, and my mom for always being there and supporting my time commitments to this book and many other projects. Also, thank you for going along with the crazy road-of-life and building so many memories together.

I love you all and couldn't imagine having a better family.

Biography

Michael Akopov is a software engineer with over a decade of professional development experience. He works primarily in backend web stacks such as PHP, Ruby, and Python and tinkers in other languages and stacks. Away from his day job, he enjoys writing articles, books, and building things with his hands. He hopes one day the roads of software and building intersect to create some fun robots or such.

He's worked in startups, enterprises, and government organizations, which has provided a breadth of experience and taught him many things. Early on, he focused more on growing his career and is now excited about building his own products. He's currently working on launching an uptime monitor, along with a couple of other ideas in the works. Follow him on Twitter, @makopov, to get updates on his work.

Foreword

I first released Laravel almost ten years ago. Since that time, over a dozen packages and services have been added to the Laravel ecosystem, helping developers with everything from social authentication to serverless deployments. An overview of this ecosystem has been sorely needed. I'm thrilled to see Michael provide a survey of the Laravel world so that developers can learn more about the variety of tools available to them.

I hope this book helps you on your journey to building your own amazing applications using Laravel. Once you've finished reading these pages, I'm confident you will have a solid understanding of our growing ecosystem and, since many of these tools are open-source, may even contribute to them yourself someday. Working together, we can all ensure a wonderful future for Laravel and PHP.

– Taylor Otwell, January 2021

Chapter

1

Introduction

Today, it seems like anyone can start a successful business with little effort. Turnkey solutions exist for many industries. For example, building a website no longer requires paying exorbitant pricing for a dev shop to make you a custom solution with custom photos and hours of development time. Services like Wix, WordPress, and many others have enabled small business owners with no development knowledge to launch a website in a matter of days. In the ecommerce industry, Shopify has become the de-facto platform for launching an online store. These services have a commonality; they make it easy for anyone to get started and produce quick results. But the trick with any business is acquiring and keeping customers. Throughout history, we can see countless examples of products that flourish as a direct result of the community and ecosystem that it is built around. You may often encounter products and platforms that are not ideal or subpar quality but find yourself having to use them because of the massive ecosystem it amassed.

This book walks through several of these examples and then shows you how Laravel can help you take an idea and leverage the powerful ecosystem to build your business and product.

Laravel's Ecosystem

Laravel is a widely popular MVC framework within the PHP community, but not merely because of its great community base. It is also a feature-rich framework that makes it very simple for a developer to create a modern web application.

While Laravel is a great framework, it won't be the primary purpose of this book. Like many great products and services that have come before, we focus on what makes Laravel continue to thrive: its ecosystem and the community built around it. We'll begin by discussing the two W's, starting with the "what." Specifically, what Laravel is, how it functions at a high level, what makes it tick, and what contributes to its popularity. We'll then discuss why you'd want to use Laravel. Next, we'll move into the many packages and services that come from the Laravel team and how you can uniquely leverage them to help you build a business. We'll then discuss how both entrepreneurs and enterprise developers can leverage many of Laravels offerings to develop better products, regardless if it's for themselves or their company. And we'll finish off by discussing some of the third party developers and package maintainers that help make the Laravel community exceptional.

In the iconic words of the late Steve Jobs, "there is one more thing." This book isn't intended just for Laravel or PHP developers. This book shows you how to leverage this ecosystem to launch your business or side project off the ground. Many of us have ideas and projects we want to create and share with the world, but few of us ever do. Frequently, we find ourselves dealing with obstacles that are not central to your business, such as framework decisions, building and maintaining servers, graphic designs, and social networking presence. All of these things are required for your business to become successful, but none of them are what people will actually be paying for. Sometimes these barriers can prevent us from ever seeing the fruit of our work. Most people who start businesses do it as a side project, in the evenings, in between classes, after the kids are in bed. Whatever your situation may be, you can not afford to worry about things outside of your core idea. Leveraging the tools in this book will help you stay on track and focused on your product.

Being an Entrepreneur

As I write this book, we are in the middle of a global pandemic, and the most uncertain times many of us have collectively faced. In the midst of these times, I've seen people go through vastly different experiences. For some, nothing has changed. Others have had their businesses prosper, while most were deeply impacted. I've seen many people launching or trying to launch their product or learn a new skill during their newly found time, and I genuinely hope they succeed. During all this, one thing became much more apparent than ever before. It's something I've heard many times and most recently read in a book. If you focus on developing, building, and acquiring assets, those assets will work for you over time. The trick, of course, is discerning what's an asset and what's a liability. Most entrepreneurs have the spirit of building and creating something most people don't even think about. But they know how to visualize these assets, and they also learned the first rule of running anything—delegate. Delegation can be anything from having the kids help clean the house to managing an assembly line. It can be seen everywhere—ultimately you're improving efficiency.

This book shows you how to delegate the problems that most software entrepreneurs face. Yet most entrepreneurs fall into the trap of focusing on the wrong issues or paying for labor they cannot afford. This book shows you how to leverage the services in Laravel's ecosystem to help you delegate.

Throughout this book, I reference six rules I've defined to lean on when making difficult decisions. I'll introduce them one by one through various scenarios and examples. I've found these rules help me make better decisions when trying to focus and hone in on a particular challenge. Business owners have to wear more hats than full-stack developers are used to. As developers, we like to give ourselves credit for being able to prioritize work and be rock stars at work.

When you're on your own, the reality of it is a very different one than when you're in company. Thoughts echo louder in an empty room. You find them coming back at you to question you when you least expect it. You quickly begin to realize you haven't been far enough around the kettle to ever see the handle. But it's OK because you're not alone. Everyone starts there, and everyone has an overwhelming number of questions.

These rules I've created are not here to avoid the vast amounts of information you don't yet know. Instead, they pose the right questions, after which you can search for the correct answer. A full head can leave you with empty pockets, while at the same time, an empty head has no pockets to worry about. Discerning what is relevant is a life skill that takes years to develop. If you're in the position to hire a mentor, do it. Find the right person to mentor you and your business, and it'll pay dividends for years to come. Until then, I encourage you to apply these rules.

> *Rule 1: Go with what you know*
>
> *Rule 2: Focus on what's important*
>
> *Rule 3: Delegate, even the things you do know*
>
> *Rule 4: Pay attention*
>
> *Rule 5: Don't jump ahead*
>
> *Rule 6: Let your customers drive your feature set*

Got an Idea?

Even a vague speckle of an idea can be enough to go off of. We've all sat at the dinner table with friends and family, throwing around ideas for a great new invention or app. The majority of us shrug them off. Sure, most of them are probably eccentric and out of reach. But there is likely an idea that's stuck around in your head for some time. One that you just can't get out of your head. It may not be a worthwhile business idea, but it's certainly worth exploring a little.

I like to explore a business idea by filling in the Lean Canvas chart[1]. The people at Lean Stack have created a one-page canvas that can help you brainstorm and put together a concise business plan to help you legitimize your idea. It breaks up the page into sections such as the problem, solution, unique value add, customer segments, channels, cost structure, key metrics, unfair advantage, and revenue stream. Take some time to complete the canvas. As you fill in each of these boxes, it forces you to think about things beyond the initial dinner table idea.

---

[1]   *Lean Canvas chart: https://leanstack.com/leancanvas*

Once you've filled in the canvas, take that canvas and review it with a few people. A spouse is a great person to start with, but they tend to support you no matter what. Try some friends who will be critical but honest. You don't want overly optimistic people, but you definitely don't need people that never see opportunity. Gather feedback, make improvements to the canvas. It's OK to do this several times and spend a week texting or emailing back and forth with people. If you find yourself looking for people to help brainstorm with you, , the community you live in likely has a business accelerator that offers programs for this very situation. I encourage you to lean into that (pun intended).

After filling out the canvas, it's generally a good idea to research the competition. You should see what they are already doing, try them out if you can, and become a customer of theirs—document everything you observe. Doing so helps

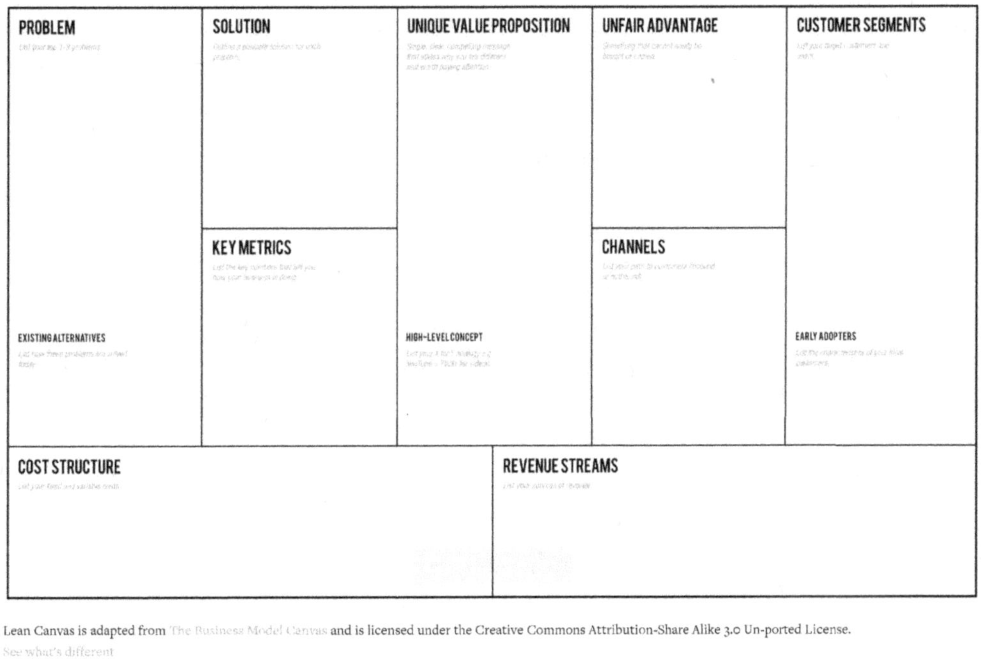

Figure 1.1.

you in building your product. There will be many things they do right. Knowing the competition helps you set yourself apart. In the book *The Art of War*, Sun Tzu writes:

> *If you know the enemy and know yourself, you need not fear the result of a hundred battles. If you know yourself but not the enemy, for every victory gained you will also suffer a defeat. If you know neither the enemy nor yourself, you will succumb in every battle.*

This advice carries over to business practice as well.

Not every business idea needs to be revolutionary or new. There are many industries with underserved users or ones that are ready for a disruption. If you find yourself experiencing a pain point in some aspect of your life, then you might be onto a business idea! Sure the market may be saturated, but at least you know it's proven, you're no longer convincing people of the market but rather why they should go with you. Companies like Uber had to prove to people that they needed a personal chauffeur and prove themselves as a company at the same time. However, if you decided to jump into ride-sharing tomorrow, I would bet many people would welcome a change to the industry norm. You'd just have to set yourself apart.

There are many ways to come up with a business idea, and one thing is certain: people worldwide are full of great ideas. I often wonder how many great ideas were taken to the grave, never given a chance to flourish. If you have a desire, the worst thing you can do is never give it a chance.

Frequently we write all the code in the world for someone else. All the while, thinking about problems in the shower, in the morning, during our commute, and in the evenings. All to make someone else rich. You might be an excellent Laravel developer, but your skills are bettering someone else and building someone else an asset that'll generate revenue.

Step out of your comfort zone. To begin with, carve out 15 minutes a day. Go ahead and have lunch with that friend. Put the idea on paper. Do the research and go beyond Laravel to see what greater purpose this tool can serve. It won't cost you anything to go beyond just the code to look at the broader picture. You might just like what you see!

Chapter

2

The Who and the What

Virtually anyone can use Laravel as a framework to develop a website or an API to power any app without reimplementing many of the basics such as authentication, database abstraction, job queueing, middleware, and scaffolding. To quote the website directly, Laravel is "The PHP Framework for Web Artisans." I believe this to be true. Many of Laravel's solutions, implementations, and internal code are written very clean, neat, and sustainable. It's crafted as a form of art.

The Who

Laravel has gained immense popularity with many different sorts of developers, and my observation is that Laravel is more popular outside of the US. I've seen developer communities and clusters popping up worldwide, from the Middle East, South East Asia, Europe, and Africa. Lagos, in particular, has a large Laravel community base. The international adoption of Laravel speaks volumes about the type of culture, community, and extensive documentation that Laravel has developed over the years. Laravel is a universal language!

It's fascinating to see the various cultures and nations adopting Laravel. What's been more interesting is seeing a commonality in the multiple categories of developers that exist. Regardless of the country, language, or problems each developer faces, there are always these sorts of developers using Laravel. These are certainly not the only types of developers out there, but I believe this covers a wide range of them. I bet if you're reading this book, you can resonate with one of them. Let's dive into them a little deeper.

Web Artisans

First, I have the already mentioned web artisans, those that enjoy this clean feeling code, minimalistic on the surface yet capable. They want well thought out processes and standards and relish the feeling of reducing ten lines of code into five lines. As a result, they gravitate towards Laravel, which provides this semblance. You will also find these developers playing around with other languages such as Ruby over Python, or Vue.js over React. I'd even go as far as to say these developers typically use Apple devices over Android or Windows.

Laravel, at its core, is built in this way. Clean syntax is always sought after. Complicated and convoluted code is a smell and not tolerated. You'll often see solutions emerging in the Laravel community because there isn't a useful or clean solution to begin with. Laravel Valet is a direct byproduct of this. We'll dive more into Valet in later chapters. If you're this type of person, the mentality and culture of Laravel will resonate with you. It goes a long way towards being productive. You'll naturally gravitate towards code that is more consistent with framework standards and, therefore, easier to maintain, write, and test.

Makers

The second type of person is a maker—the person who just needs a tool, a feature-rich MVC framework in a language they're familiar with. They don't have much of an opinion on tools, and they only recognize what each one can accomplish and then set out to do their job. The great thing about Laravel is that it offers many of the solutions and integrations a modern framework would need, enabling people to build modern websites rapidly. Laravel features a best in class background job queuing system and unified notification support across a multitude of channels such as WebSockets, Slack, email, text, and more.

If you're a maker, you're likely more excited about the various capabilities of Laravel more than anything else. You quickly see how you can leverage its many features and functions to solve specific problems that you predict you'll have or that you've had in the past. This diversity is a great strength to have, and you can leverage this knowledge to problem solve in your application.

You're probably pretty good at executing solutions to problems at work or home. I'm willing to bet you enjoy making and building outside of work as well. I often see these types of individuals doing woodworking or some other form of hands-on building outside of work, probably with a garage full of tools.

I fall into this category, though I've pushed myself to leverage the strengths of the other two types over the years. I love to make things. I love seeing a product come together, leveraging various tools together to see a product through. The flip side to this is that it's easy to get caught up in the tools and build process that you forget to look at the bigger picture, the roadmap, the customers that will use this. You may forget to ask yourself, "Why am I building this? Who will use it? How can I provide more value to the customer with this?"

These skills take time to learn. However, the Laravel ecosystem can help free up some of your time and mental burden from day-to-day operations that will likely distract you. For example, I have built many deployment and server provisioning pipelines over the years. Still, for my personal projects, instead of getting distracted by assembling something I've done many times for others, I signed up for Laravel Vapor and never worry about infrastructure or deployment again. This decision offsets the mentality of "I've built that before, I can do it better." You have a smooth CI/CD pipeline before you know it, but it's deploying a broken application that no one needs.

Throughout these chapters, keep an eye out for tools you can leverage to avoid the pitfall I just described. For me, it was deploying and server management. For you, it might be something different. Whatever it is, there is likely a solution in the community that can help keep you on track.

Entrepreneur

The third type of person and one that I often see gravitate towards Laravel is the entrepreneur. This could be for many reasons. Sure, they could also be web artisans at heart, or only looking for a tool, or looking for the next hot thing that's easy to hire for. However, I believe there is another reason they choose Laravel—the core values that Laravel was built on. Laravel and its packages were produced as a tool to build a software company. It's a tool built with business and entrepreneurship in mind, and, as we'll see throughout the course of this book, Laravel has fostered an ecosystem of business, entrepreneurship, and results. The framework itself is used by Taylor Otwell himself to run his business. As a result, much of this ecosystem has been noticed and adopted by those with the same spirit and the same drive—those who want to craft something beautiful, dependable, and extendable.

If you haven't already, you'll fall in love with Laravel's ecosystem of like-minded individuals. Even as you read the documentation, you'll find that the examples provided are usually real business examples. For example, the event system used e-commerce terms such as "an order was placed," and "order was paid, now let's send off an email." These examples are quite relatable and should make quick work of trying to solve prevalent problems.

Some people don't fall directly into one or any of these categories. I now fall into all three categories, and that's perfectly OK. This isn't a box meant to trap you, but rather a way for you to glean your current strengths and biases so you can be on the lookout for what will help you the most as you dive into this journey.

The What

Sometimes the best way to answer the why is to look at "the what." If you already know what Laravel is, you may skip to the <u>next section</u>. But for those of you who are not as familiar, there's no reason to worry. We'll walk through this together.

Laravel is an MVC framework (Model, View, Controller), but that only describes how Laravel is structured at a high level. MVC frameworks separate the parts of your application into the data (Models), display screens or pages (Views), and logic that accepts user input and does something with it (Controller). This section will briefly cover some of the key components that make Laravel so great. Let's start with the view layer.

Blade Templates

Laravel ships with its own DSL for creating views and front end templates called Blade[1]. Blade is similar to PHP in syntax but provides many useful functions for manipulating data at the presentation layer. It is still rendered server-side and sent as HTML to the browser. Blade allows you to structure your code to develop a set of reusable components, pages, and layouts. Doing so is essential as it will enable you to reuse code across your app. For example, you might have a notification alert that opens up to prompt the user. Instead of copying this code to every page where it might appear, you can write it in one file and include it everywhere you need. This practice allows for the deduplication of code and easier development with only one file to modify.

With native support for localization, you can adapt the same template for any geographical region. Laravel also ships with Blade UI scaffolding for your most basic pages such as a landing page, log in, registration, password reset, and a welcome page for authenticated users. The use of this scaffolding is entirely optional. But with native support for View.js and React, you may find these scaffold files are an excellent starting point.

Laravel's view layer supports many cool things, most of which we'll cover in later chapters. One additional feature I'd like you to be aware of is that Laravel supports push notifications out of the box utilizing either the pusher[2] service or a hosted

---

[1]   Blade: <u>https://laravel.com/docs/8.x/blade</u>
[2]   pusher: <u>https://pusher.com</u>

Redis server or socket.io[3]. This feature allows you to construct a web page that can notify the user whenever some backend state changes. Perhaps your client has ordered food, and it is ready for pickup; you can notify them right in the browser without requiring them to reload the page.

Eloquent

Much like how Blade lets us present data to the user, Eloquent allows us to store and retrieve data from different database providers to our application consistently. Eloquent is commonly known as an ORM, or Object-Relational Mapping[4]. An ORM's primary purpose is to provide a consistent and easy to use way of defining your data objects in code that maps to a database schema. To the consumer, it's agnostic of which database you're using. It can be PostgreSQL or MySQL, and Eloquent handles the differences between the two, not the developer.

If we have an e-commerce platform, we could have one Eloquent object for orders and another for customers. We also need to represent the relationship between the two. We know that an order is associated with a single customer. However, a single customer can have many orders. We usually define this relationship in the database with a foreign key reference from the `orders` table to the primary key on the `customers` table in a column usually named `customer_id`. With this database setup done at the migration level, Eloquent only needs to know that an order `belongsTo` a customer and that a customer `hasMany` orders. Now when loading a customer's dashboard, you can quickly gather all their orders with one call: `$customer->orders()`. It returns all of the orders assigned to that customer.

Eloquent's abilities are nearly endless, it seems. Yet, there's always something to learn with Eloquent. If you're looking to make your database queries performant or you need to perform some complex queries, take the time and read the Eloquent documentation[5] at length. If you're looking for more optimizations beyond just the docs, you should follow the work of Jonathan Reinink[6]. He has excellent write-ups on Eloquent performance improvements on his website and Twitter account,

---

[3]   socket.io: https://socket.io
[4]   Object-Relational Mapping: https://en.wikipedia.org/wiki/Object-relational_mapping
[5]   Eloquent documentation: https://laravel.com/docs/8.x/eloquent
[6]   Jonathan Reinink: https://reinink.ca

@reinink. He recently launched a book titled *Eloquent Performance Patterns*[7] that collects many of his tips and tricks and is a worthwhile investment.

Controllers

Laravel's controller layer helps with authenticating, handling, and routing requests, much like any other framework. You can even split up your controllers for API based requests and view based requests. Much of the authentication is taken care of for you through Laravel's auth middleware, but the middleware doesn't have to be just for authentication. You could expand it for authorization. If you have roles in your application and need to make sure the person accessing a route is authorized to see that page, this would be a great place to place that check. While we can and should utilize many architectural concepts as you build your application, I'd like to showcase a couple of key concepts here.

> **Authentication versus Authorization**
>
> *These two concepts are often used interchangeably and work closely together. But in a web application, they refer to separate ideas. Authentication means verifying someone is whom they say they are. Authorization refers to checking that a user is allowed to perform some task in your application.*

The first one being Laravel's internal event listener. Event listeners are known conceptually as pub/sub systems, or publisher/subscriber[8]. In essence, your application may post an event to the system, and other components can listen for such events. For example, you may have an e-commerce process that posts an OrderComplete message. Once this message is available to the system, other parts of the application can subscribe to this event and be notified when it happens so that they can do what they need to. Such a system is very flexible because components can emit or listen to events without knowing much about how other parts of the application work.

Going back to our e-commerce application, once an order is complete, you may want to send an email to the customer with confirmation of their order. You may also choose to notify some administration service or company slack. The user's order

---

[7] *Eloquent Performance Patterns:* https://eloquent-course.reinink.ca
[8] *publisher/subscriber:* https://en.wikipedia.org/wiki/Publish–subscribe_pattern

also needs to be fulfilled and shipped. You'll need to assign it to the correct distribution center if you have multiple. If you offer rewards for purchases, you want to update the user's profile with the correct rewards points. All of these events need to happen as soon as you have an order purchased and completed, but they certainly don't need to happen synchronously on the main thread of the request your user made. There is no need to hold up the user any longer than required. You can show them their confirmation page as soon as you've confirmed payment.

Laravel allows for a coherent and clean solution for registering many listeners to events. You might be wondering how you could execute these in a background job, as I mentioned before. Laravel makes this as straightforward as extending the listener class with a implements ShouldQueue. This interface is all it takes for Laravel to queue up the event listener and run it in a background job. The ShouldQueue interface tells Laravel that this object is queueable, and it treats it like any other queued object.

Queues

This brings me to my favorite feature of Laravel, background queues. Straight out of the box, Laravel ships with a built-in queuing mechanism. This mechanism allows you to easily connect Laravel with several different types of queue drivers such as Redis, Amazon SQS, and even the application database for small queues or development. Once you connect to a driver, you can run your background queues with an artisan command, and off they go, working in the background the silent workhorse of your application.

On the application side of things, Laravel provides a queueable class interface for use in Jobs[9], Notifications[10] and Mailable's[11] as the primary use case. At the bare minimum, you must extend the class to implement ShouldQueue to queue a job. Laravel will now know to process this job out of the main thread and in a background queue. There are a ton of configuration options when enqueuing your job. The flexibility of the system makes it my favorite aspect of the framework.

---

[9]   Jobs: *https://laravel.com/docs/8.x/queues#creating-jobs*
[10] Notifications: *https://laravel.com/docs/8.x/notifications#introduction*
[11] Mailable's: *https://laravel.com/docs/8.x/mail#generating-mailables*

What You'll Need

This section is for those who have either never done development before or are new to Laravel development in particular. Getting started with Laravel development is straightforward. First, you need a system capable of running a small web server and database. Most modern systems are capable of this, and 8GB of memory should suffice with some extra local disk space. We'll run through several options for doing local development in the coming chapters. However, I would warn you that if your system is light on resources, you may benefit from using a Docker-based setup for doing development. Containers are much less resource-intensive than running a virtual machine (VM). In the end, you should experiment and see what works best for you.

You'll also need a text editor or IDE (Integrated Development Environment). Microsoft's Visual Studio Code is a free and good quality editor. Make sure you are using a text editor and not a word processor. PHP's interpreter works with plain-text files.

After you have an editor selected, you should install Git[12] to help you with committing your code to a repository. Git is useful for tracking changes to your application's code. Without it, you're likely to clutter your directories with old copies "just in case."

Next comes the challenge of actually running the PHP code. The best place to start this is on the Laravel getting started guides[13]. I provide an excellent summary of these various starting guides in the local development chapter. I suggest reading through these before deciding where to start from as Laravel offers several different local development options.

---

[12] Git: *https://git-scm.com/book/en/v2/Getting-Started-Installing-Git*
[13] getting started guides: *https://laravel.com/docs/8.x/installation*

Chapter

3

About The Ecosystem

Many of the neat features I've described to you in earlier chapters might begin to paint a picture of why I enjoy working with Laravel so much. However, after creating, maintaining, inheriting, and eventually decommissioning many projects over the years, I've come to realize something about the many projects I've had (the privilege?) to decommission over the years.

Many of the projects I've replaced or simply retired over the years were because they became difficult to maintain. Usually, it was due to poorly written code compounded over the years, causing extremely long development times. Delays arose because it was difficult to test anything, or updates caused breaking changes just about every time anything changed. Eventually, someone decided this project was too expensive to maintain and that it would be cheaper to gut it and start fresh. Frequently I would hear the blame being passed down to the language or framework. In reality though, it was rarely the fault of the tools used, likely an inexperienced developer abusing the choice of tooling. Other reasons were the project was built on something that no one knew how to code in anymore. Whether it was a language that was no longer popular or a framework that never caught on except outside a select few who no longer worked at the company. Sometimes, the framework and the language could be very well known, but no one in your organization, aside from a handful, knows how to code in it.

Working with Rails

I'll give you an example. I worked for an employer not too long ago with an abundant mix of projects for various agencies as well as R&D focus areas. Each project was unique and challenging in its way. My favorite aspect of working there was that each of these projects would be in a different language or framework. They could be hosted on-premise or in the cloud. Sometimes you were assigned to new projects, and these were fun. You got to pick what you wrote it in, how you shaped it, and what CI/CD to use. It was as if you had a baby project of your own. As a research organization, they supported anything as long as it got the research done.

One day I was approached there and asked if I wanted to be on a project that had been around for several years. It was well funded, well known, and needed more developers. In fact, they had a difficult time finding developers that knew this framework and would work on it. I was a little surprised to hear that but figured it was another niche framework that some Ph.D. students created to impress their professors. I asked what the framework was, not thinking much of it. "Ruby on Rails," the project manager said to me. I was shocked, Ruby on Rails[1] is a well-known framework, and some of the biggest sites are written in Rails. Rails fundamentally shifted the way the modern web was developed.

---

[1] Ruby on Rails: https://rubyonrails.org

Before Rails, many developers rolled their own standards for nearly every project, or they would write some authentication mechanism and try to port it over to every project they did. They were creating a series of spaghetti code that was similar and yet different between applications. Then, along came Rails offering an opinionated way to build web applications, and many people loved having a set of rules to follow. It handled authentication and authorization consistently across each project. Rails also made it very easy to communicate with your database of choice, creating one of the most popular ORM's to exist. Back end developers were able to write front end views using a simple scripting language dynamically. This simple approach revolutionized how we developed websites. You could spin up a functioning website overnight. And yet, at this organization, we had few people—you could count them on one hand—able to write in this framework, especially at such a diverse organization.

I was no exception to that rule. I had never worked with Rails before. Years ago, I dug into it for a couple of weeks, back when it was gaining traction with Rails 2. I learned some basic ruby scripting and then never touched it again after going back to university from my summer break. I had enjoyed it and wanted to continue learning, but nothing pressing made it a priority. Like all things, it was shelved for another day. So I decided to join this project. I actually ended up being a part of it for over two years by supporting this application and learning Ruby and the Rails framework. Working in an R&D facility, sometimes the way you approach code solutions is very ad hoc. Working in a framework with structure was excellent. With the vast community support and packages, finding solutions to common problems to help me focus on the task at hand was effortless. Had I not joined this project, and we could not find another developer to assist in the project, it's entirely possible that this project would have also collapsed or been awarded to another organization.

That Rails project came close to death, but others, they met it face to face. I've had to retire many MediaWiki, Joomla, custom frameworks, and other sites simply because no one used the frameworks anymore. They didn't have enough support or active development around them to keep the momentum going. Various reasons made them an unacceptable choice for long term maintainability. I've listed out several reasons that I've seen projects fail down below. Many of these projects get created and then handed off to someone else to figure out what to do with, so choosing a framework that is popular or easy to learn is always preferred from a management perspective.

> - *Years of lousy design decisions compounding together*
> - *Bandaid implementations that punt off tech debt work*
> - *Extremely long development time due to technical debt and other design decisions*
> - *Overly complicated application, not broken down enough, or doing too much*
> - *Choosing to "roll our own" instead of a community implementation*
> - *Lack of developers with necessary skills to maintain the project*
> - *Unpopular framework or language causing small talent pool*

Discovering Laravel

When I was learning Ruby on Rails, I learned of this interesting PHP framework many developers were gloating about at conferences. I remember one of the discussions at ZendCon whether it was pronounced "Lara-vel" or "Lar-a-vel". Either way, everyone thought it was fantastic. The Collections class alone streamlined working with arrays and objects as a standard iterator for both made iterating over vast amounts of data enjoyable. I had to know more. After all, I spent a large portion of my career at this point writing PHP code, Drupal, Joomla, custom frameworks. I had to see what was so elegant about this framework.

I began by sitting through a couple of presentations on the framework. I watched videos online, and then I thought I'd give it a shot. Immediately I was taken back by the sheer quality of documentation. It wasn't auto-generated docs from annotation blocks. It was well written, thought out, laid out, and explained using coherent sentences made for human beings instead of T1000 terminators from the future.

Diving into Laravel around the same time that I was learning Rails was quite splendid. I've done this twice in my life now, where I worked in both Rails and Laravel. Many of the concepts are the same, although there are some things each framework is constrained due to the programming language specifications. Given much of the similarity of each framework, you might be wondering, "Well, why not just use Rails then?" It seems to be more attractive on a resume compared to PHP.

To which I answer, "you're probably right." It's no secret that PHP has received a bad reputation in the programming world, and honestly, rightly so. While PHP may have innovated many of the original server-side implementations of web technologies, it has undoubtedly left a lot to be desired in recent years. PHP turned into a wild west in many ways while other languages were slowly gaining traction on the web. For example, Ruby was predominantly used for scripting and automation. Python was used—and still is—for machine learning, automation, and all sorts of data manipulation.

In comparison, PHP was built specifically for the web. It had no real concept of what objects and object-oriented programming would become, nor did it care. These were websites, after all, not real software!

Fast forward to today, and PHP has now implemented many of the raving features other languages offer. With version 8 out now, it'll continue that trend of keeping pace with the other big players by offering even more enhancements than PHP7 offered—my favorite of which is the addition of a JIT compiler. But even with all of these additions to the language, PHP still has a bad reputation. I've heard countless times in recent years, "you still use PHP?", "I thought PHP was dead," or "I didn't think anyone used PHP still." Despite all the hard work by the community, PHP will likely continue to have a bad reputation.

Honestly, if your biggest concern is being hirable at a moment's notice, you should find a different language for yourself. Stack Overflow releases its list of most popular programming languages every year. Even though PHP still powers some 80% of all internet sites, it ranks relatively low in many of the comprehensive lists put together by such organizations.

You might be wondering, "Uh, Michael, I thought you were supposed to be selling me on Laravel. Why are you telling me PHP is not a hirable language?" That's a great question. The purpose of this book is not to sell you on a language or a framework. It's to show those who are entrepreneurs at heart how the Laravel ecosystem can help you achieve many of your entrepreneurial goals. We'll dive deeper into this in later chapters.

Let's go back to why we choose Laravel over Rails or Django—or insert framework here—in the first place. In the case of these three frameworks, it's pretty straight forward. You go with whichever language you know the most. Rule #1 of starting a business, "go with what you know." Perhaps, you're sitting around the house thinking about this neat idea you have and decided you want to try and do something with it. At the same time, you've decided to learn Rails or React or whatever other thing you don't know while building a business. Stop yourself. 99.9% of the time, doing so is a terrible idea, and no, you're not the .01% exception.

Evaluate Your Goals

When you've decided to start a business, you're choosing to trade your time building a product for others to use in exchange for their money. That's it. If you start mixing in tutorials and learning something new from scratch while building a product, it's likely that you won't know the best framework solutions for what you want to do. I have found that it's best to stick to what you know when launching something you want to share with the world. Not that you shouldn't learn anything ever again. But rather than experimenting with your business, keep the two intentions separate. Launching a business pushes you to learn so much about many other things that you'll be glad you simplified where you could.

You should ask yourself if what you're after is to learn a new tool, language, or skill at this fork in the road. Or, is your goal to take that cool idea you have, share it with the world, and make some money while you're at it.

Chapter

4

Developer Tools

What truly makes Laravel unique is its ecosystem. Laravel has been consistent with its quality and usefulness of features while maintaining clean code and thorough documentation. It has led to deep trust over the years in what developers can expect from Laravel—resulting in an ecosystem consisting of core Laravel as well as third party applications and packages.

This chapter focuses on core Laravel packages that help you be productive when developing your application. Laravel offers options for building your application, environments for local development, and coding tools for boosting your productivity.

Valet

When I first learned of Valet[1], I became a very happy developer. I would argue that Valet helped me save money and extended the life of my laptop. "How?" you might ask. Before I can answer that, I have to explain what Valet is first.

Building a web application requires running your application locally, as this is the most convenient way for you to change code and see immediate results. It doesn't rely on a cloud server or an internet connection to code, making the experience much smoother for you as a developer. To do that, you'd traditionally run a Linux VM on your local system that sets up the webserver, PHP, database, cache, and other components. Ideally, you'd even provision this using an automated provisioning system such as Vagrant.

This approach is valid, and it works fine, but there are several bottlenecks with it. First, It was resource-intensive. Typically running a virtual machine required redundant overhead ram usage as you were running an entire operating system on top of your already running system. This solution meant having a system with 16GB or more of RAM to run things properly. Another drawback was having to rebuild this when things broke. I say "when" because, in a development environment, it's only a matter of time before you have to rebuild the thing from scratch. Doing so is a very time-consuming process when doing it by hand and leads to distractions and frustration.

A few years ago, a new type of service came along that I'm sure you've heard of, Docker. Docker has long been oversimplified as a lightweight virtual machine. While this somewhat describes the result of running a Docker container, it isn't an accurate representation. I would also like to take this moment to clarify that a container doesn't have to be a Docker container. The container concept has been baked into the Linux kernel. But Docker made this technology mainstream in a whole new way. You could now run an entire Linux image that was just 5MB in size. This was unheard of. By running only what you need within that container, you can minimize the file size and resource utilization without too much hassle.

Containers make use of the underlying operating system for everything that it doesn't need on its own. In fact, containers employ what is known as copy-on-write. It only creates a system file in the image if it were to differ from the host.

---

[1]   Valet: *https://laravel.com/docs/7.x/valet*

Running a set of containers is an excellent solution for replicating specific environments in a lightweight and portable fashion and works well for development. However, frequently you find that you're not changing PHP or database versions all that often. You don't need the ability to set up and tear down a container or virtual machine. Typically, to run a Laravel site, all you need is PHP, NGINX, and MySQL or PostgreSQL. These services can run natively on any operating system. Traditionally, setting all of these up on a desktop system such as Windows or even MacOS is a pain. Sure, you can do it with Vagrant, but you're still scripting all of this.

Here is where Valet comes in. Valet is the brainchild of Adam Wathan and Taylor Otwell. They decided that running a VM or a set of containers was simply overkill for running a basic Laravel site. So they built Valet, a service that runs on a Mac and configures a webserver with all of the PHP connections and DNS routing necessary to serve a website.

Valet makes it very easy to turn any PHP website directory into a hosted site locally by running a `valet link` command. Valet automatically detects what framework your site is written in. Did I mention Valet supports many PHP based frameworks outside of Laravel? That's right. I even use it for Drupal 7 and 8 development. After detecting your framework, it configures the necessary routes to your `index.php` file, after which your site is available at the domain `http://{site_dir_name}.test`.

You're still required to install PHP and MySQL or PostgreSQL separately through either Homebrew or some other way, but everything else is configured automatically. This approach allows a very lightweight and minimal installation on your Mac, which is great for battery life and local development.

Valet ships with all sorts of useful features, and there are a few worth pointing out that are likely to benefit every user of Valet. Sometimes, you want or need to run your local development site via SSL. Valet makes this as straightforward as running `valet secure` within the directory of your site. After it runs, you will notice that it's secured with a TLS connection when you visit your site. You should see the HTTPS lock icon in your browser.

One thing I find myself often doing—being a remote developer (especially under quarantine)—is wanting to share the status or current state of my site with a colleague or friend to get some quick feedback. Valet makes this possible by running the valet share command, which uses ngrok[2] to create a tunnel and displays a shareable URL that allows access from the outside world into your system.

Valet offers other helpful features that are worth exploring in the docs[3]. Valet's one downside is that it's only usable by Mac users. There are attempts by community members to create a Microsoft Windows equivalent of Valet. I've never needed to use them, so I cannot speak on their behalf.

Homestead

While Valet is a great resource for Mac users, it isn't the right fit for everyone. If you're a Windows, Linux, or even a Mac user that prefers to keep their system free of any configuration mess, you may consider Homestead[4] instead. Homestead is a virtual machine setup by the Laravel community that is preconfigured with everything needed to run a Laravel site.

I've built and used many virtual machines over the years. I have to admit that Homestead is a very well put together virtual machine. Aside from merely running a site with SSL, it offers several powerful features that make developing a site locally quick and convenient. For example, it allows developers to set up automatic backups of development databases and database snapshots using LVM, which allows for fast restores. This is handy if you need to test a dataset then restore your database to a previous point in time.

Like Valet, Homestead also supports other frameworks and site types beyond Laravel, which is valuable when working with various other projects. One feature most of us would make use of is the out-of-the-box setup of Mailhog within Homestead. Valet doesn't ship with an equivalent solution. If you're like me and prefer to use Valet, you're probably using a third-party mail catch service to test your development emails. However, with Mailhog being built-in to Homestead, there is one less reason to need an internet connection, which is nice for those camping trips.

---

[2] ngrok: https://ngrok.com
[3] docs: https://laravel.com/docs/8.x/valet
[4] Homestead: https://laravel.com/docs/7.x/homestead

It's best to have your local environment match the production setup as closely as possible to reduce surprises and unexpected errors. While Homestead can't possibly predict your exact production environment, it makes some assumptions as well as offers extensibility. For example, you can change between six different versions of PHP, starting at 5.6. You can also switch the default web server from NGINX to Apache if that's what you prefer. In fact, changing web servers is as easy as SSHing into the VM and running `flip`. Simple is elegant.

To assist in debugging your application, Homestead ships with Xdebug preconfigured. Sometimes, you'll need to configure your `xdebug.ini` file, but the default configuration should "just work" for the most part. For more in-depth profiling of your application, you can utilize Blackfire[5] and XHGui[6], both of which come preconfigured within Homestead.

Homestead offers many features and advantages over running anything on your machine or setting up custom virtual machines or containers. The amount of time needed to set a proper working system is very time-consuming. This doesn't even consider the amount of time required to maintain a system. Testing different PHP versions can also be a hassle. With Homestead, you can do this in a matter of minutes. While I use Valet to avoid running a virtual machine, I certainly consider Homestead invaluable. As an aspiring entrepreneur, Homestead offers you the perfect development environment to get up and running while focusing on Rule 2, and for some of us less technical, Rule 1 as well.

---

[5]   Blackfire: https://www.blackfire.io
[6]   XHGui: https://github.com/perftools/xhgui

Sail

Laravel Sail[7] is the latest package to join the Laravel ecosystem. Sail is a docker-based local development environment that spins up PHP/Nginx, MySQL, Redis, and Mailhog containers. With the PHP container, you can pick which version of PHP you'd want it to spin up. By default, it runs version 8. Running a Docker container locally is a light way method for getting up and running quickly. Containers require fewer resources to run compared to VMs, and they are ephemeral by nature. If your system crashes or breaks, you can always kill it and spin up a brand new development environment within minutes.

Since Sail is based on Docker, you are free to customize any of the services or Docker files as you wish. You can modify the `docker-compose.yml` and the appropriate `Dockerfile` to install whatever service you need and then rebuild your containers.

Right after installing Sail, you have a new file called `docker-compose.yml`. This file defines what services Docker should start and with what parameters. This is essentially in place of running the commands by hand `docker run php/php7 --volumes…` You see how this can become tedious to do. Docker Compose offers a simple YAML definition that you can use to spin up the same containers each time by running `docker-compose up`. In Laravel Sail's case, we run the command `sail up`, which proxies the appropriate commands to Docker. Running the `up` command will build and spin up all containers defined in the `.yml` file. The Dockerfile that it builds from is located within the Composer `vendor/` directory. If you'd like to modify it, you should first run this command:

```
php artisan sail:publish
```

Doing so copies the Docker files to the root of your application directory so you can modify them.

Containers are a great way to develop because they are lightweight and reproducible and because containers are portable. Using them, you can follow a similar build process to deploy your application to production, making it easy to ship. I have an article on this titled Containerizing Production PHP[8] that I encourage you to

---

[7]   Laravel Sail: https://laravel.com/docs/8.x/sail
[8]   Containerizing Production PHP: https://www.phparch.com/article/containerizing-production-php/

read if you're interested in learning more about how to move a Docker-based PHP application to production. Another benefit of using Docker-based containers is that all developers at your organization can use identical development environments by checking in the Docker files.

Laravel Sail is a worthwhile addition to the ecosystem. Many people have been running their versions of Docker-based development environments—I have. However, having an officially supported package is an excellent addition.

Choosing a Local Development Setup

Choosing a development environment can be a difficult decision for many developers. It often is a very personal decision in how developers set up their system. Such is the case with terminal setups or IDE color configurations. However, choosing which color and font to use is different than how your code should run. Ultimately what you want when running your code is an environment as closely similar to your production environment as possible—matching PHP versions, identical web server, matching PHP packages, and a matching database provider and version are at a minimum necessary. By matching development to production, you're less likely to be surprised by something that breaks or works differently when deployed. It's critical when your production environment is a container setup with many containers talking to each other. You'll want to test out the cross container communication locally before deploying. Beyond that, not as much matters. However, there are other considerations to take based on my own experiences.

I've gone over several local development options that are available directly from the Laravel community. There is a local install option, virtual machine, or a Docker-based version. At the end of the day, they all work. You should try out all of these options to see what works best for you. The Valet option is ideal for resource-constrained systems where the largest gains are achieved by running a web server and PHP natively. I've used this setup for years, and it's effortless, especially on a Mac. It also requires minimal setup or maintenance.

On the flip side, if you prefer to treat your infrastructure as ephemeral, you'll want the ability to reproduce it quickly. For this, consider using a container-based setup such as Docker. Docker allows you to define exactly how your images are built and requires little additional overhead to run beyond the code itself. Container images can be pre-built and re-run instantly. This setup works well if you have a team of engineers and you prefer to port your environment around to all engineers. If your production environment runs in a container setup such as Kubernetes, using containers to develop locally helps you mimic production most closely. This setup requires a single command to spin up. While this setup is very portable and reproducible, your code should be just as portable and reproducible. It will require special considerations such as using relative paths and storing files in S3 or another offsite storage. You'll also want to have well-functioning migrations and seeder files. That way, you can reproduce your local setup instantly and consistently.

A last possible setup is a virtual machine, which provides you with little to no setup, and a huge slew of features out of the box with Homestead. This solution is just as reproducible as a container. Still, it is slower and requires noticeably more computing resources than a container since it runs an entire system on top of your local machine. If you have the resources and don't mind running a VM, this is an excellent way to get many features and services without installing them by hand.

There is no right or wrong tool. There is only what makes sense. I've always said, "do what makes sense, don't make sense of what you do." This advice applies to local development as much as anything else. Your needs and circumstances will vary drastically from other developers. Therefore there is no need to decide based on what someone else is doing but rather what you need. I have run all of these setups, and all have been helpful. For example, when my local Valet setup broke, I was able to fall back to Homestead and continue developing while resolving my local development environment in my spare time. I recently ran Laravel Sail to reduce the overhead of resources on my local system, an easy drop-in replacement from Homestead.

These decisions can be difficult, and while starting a new business, forces you to make millions of decisions every day—shades of blue to use, font style, and others. There is no reason to make this decision more complicated than it needs to be. Ultimately they all allow you to get started within minutes. What matters most is how you write and maintain your code, which enables it to stay portable.

Tinker

Laravel Tinker[9] is another useful tool within the Laravel arsenal for quickly evaluating Laravel code right within your console. Tinker is a REPL language shell. If you're not already familiar, REPL stands for Read-Evaluate-Print-Loop. It's a command-line tool executed within the context of the language or framework it was built for. The general execution of a REPL is as it states. It begins by "Reading" input from the user, typically a command or function call of some sort. It then "Evaluates" that code, next it "Prints" the results, and finally, it "Loops" back to the read state. If you use Bash or any similar shell, you're using a REPL.

As mentioned, Tinker is a REPL built for Laravel. You can execute it with the command:

```php
php artisan tinker
```

It drops you into a bootstrapped instance of your application. This bootstrapped state is handy for executing code and receiving immediate feedback from your application. It's similar to how you might execute code in the middle of a debug statement.

If you're already using a debugger, you may not need Tinker for everyday debugging. However, there are still use cases for it that I've come across, mainly when working on small projects. Suppose you run into issues with inconsistencies in production. In that case, you can open up a Tinker session on the server and—with extreme caution—execute commands to investigate what's going on. *Use this as a last resort, as you are working directly on the production database.* Generating one-off reports is another use case I've come across that Tinker helped with.

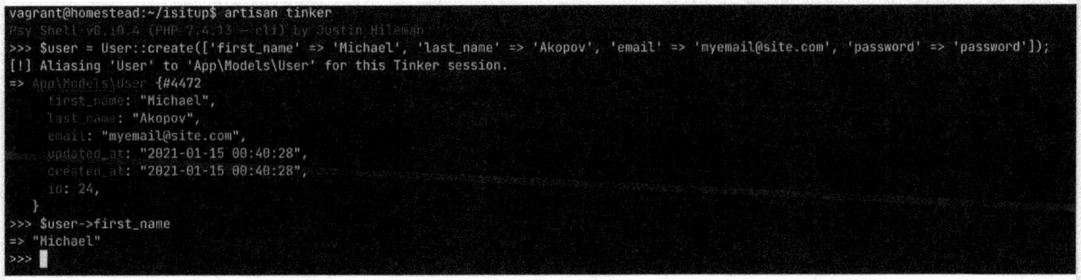

```
vagrant@homestead:~/isitup$ artisan tinker
Psy Shell v0.10.4 (PHP 7.4.13 — cli) by Justin Hileman
>>> $user = User::create(['first_name' => 'Michael', 'last_name' => 'Akopov', 'email' => 'myemail@site.com', 'password' => 'password']);
[!] Aliasing 'User' to 'App\Models\User' for this Tinker session.
=> App\Models\User {#4472
     first_name: "Michael",
     last_name: "Akopov",
     email: "myemail@site.com",
     updated_at: "2021-01-15 00:40:28",
     created_at: "2021-01-15 00:40:28",
     id: 24,
   }
>>> $user->first_name
=> "Michael"
>>>
```

Figure 4.1.

---

[9]   Laravel Tinker: https://laravel.com/docs/8.x/artisan#tinker

There are many ways to achieve the examples above. I don't advocate for any particular uses of Tinker. They are merely examples of what I've used it for. In summary, Tinker is a useful REPL tool for executing Laravel code against your application. Use it as you see best.

Telescope

Debugging comes in many forms. Many of us are familiar with the traditional method of debugging using print statements or dd in Laravel, which is short for Dump and Die. It dumps your data, then exits the application. Some of us use an Xdebug setup to set breakpoints in our application, examine the call stack, inspect variables in place, and evaluate expressions. Doing so is a great way to debug logical errors and even try out code variations during runtime. While these debugging methods are great for isolated issues, they fail to provide you with deep insights into your full application's runtime call stack. It does not tell you how many queries are performed, how many succeed, fail, or how long they take. You don't know whether your events are firing off in the correct sequence or many other runtime checks unavailable during a debug session. Instead, this is where Telescope comes in handy.

Laravel telescope is a core Laravel open-source package that continually monitors your application in the background and gathers information about each of your application's requests. Some of the data it collects includes the request payload data, specific queries executed, the models that get loaded, and even the view files used for a page request, among many more data metrics. The last one about views is one of

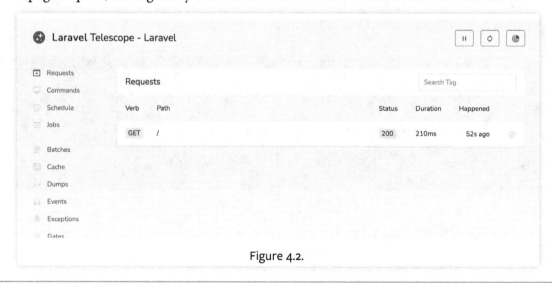

Figure 4.2.

my favorites. I'm not a very skilled front end developer, so I rely on as much boilerplate as possible. So any insight into views and where they're coming from really helps me out when trying to debug something.

You might be wondering when this would come in handy. For applications that are mainly CRUD based, Telescope likely won't provide much useful insight beyond what you could gather from a debugger. But when your application grows beyond simple operations and begins to utilize queued jobs, caches, and event listeners, it becomes increasingly more complex to verify that your application is executing in the correct order even with many processes running in parallel.

Figure 4.3.

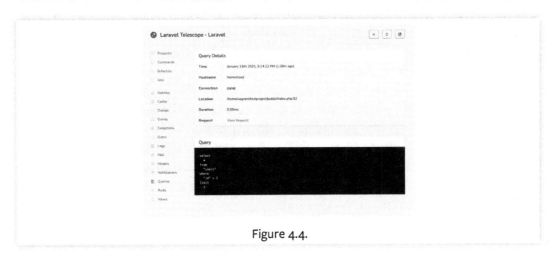

Figure 4.4.

I'll give you a short example of where this came in useful for me. I was building an uptime monitor. The system required a series of queue workers to run in the background checking if a site is up. One of the primary offerings of the monitor was that it performed specific geographic checks of the website to determine if it was down from all regions. To execute this successfully, I had to run several queued jobs for each site, each in a different geographic region. Once all the regions finished executing, I had to check the status of each and make determinations. This synchronization was only possible to achieve by utilizing an in-memory cache and Laravel's built-in event system.

As you might imagine, timing which job finished last was tricky. After all, they ran in no set order. Telescope came in handy here. I was able to run my uptime monitor on a specific site and see the exact order that various components of the system executed. After several iterations with different execution times, I determined specific patterns that led me to find some logical issues in my code. These sorts of problems are tricky to test with automation scripting, though not impossible. But that's a discussion for another time. Stay tuned.

Telescope is designed much like Laravel Horizon. It installs[10] via Composer and has a dashboard exposed at the path `/telescope`. This same dashboard is also only available to select admin users you define within the service provider class `app/Providers/TelescopeServiceProvider.php`. There are other configurable options for Telescope within the config file `config/telescope.php` that you can read more about online[11]. I generally find that the default configuration for Telescope is sufficient.

One thing to keep in mind that the online docs warn about is the amount of data that Telescope collects will quickly grow and occupy table space. To avoid bloating your database, be sure to schedule the artisan command that ships with it. This command performs housekeeping and prunes the necessary tables. Telescope also offers a pause button. If you decide you don't need any data at the moment, you can disable it. This pause button also exists because it is technically possible to run Telescope in production, and people have. This way, you can run it only when necessary. I highly advise against this as you'll more than likely deal with lots of noise in production. If you find yourself leaning towards this direction, try first to replicate the scenario locally to minimize data noise and unnecessary database costs that come with extreme logging in production.

---

[10] installs: https://laravel.com/docs/8.x/telescope#installation
[11] you can read more about online: https://laravel.com/docs/8.x/telescope#available-watchers

Dusk

Laravel Dusk is an open-source package that helps Laravel developers to build browser automation tests. Dusk out of the box utilizes a ChromeDriver. However, you're free to use any Selenium[12] based driver.

Browser-based tests are some of the most useful tests you can create for your site. They test the application from the end user's perspective. Whereas typical unit or integration tests may test specific code paths or functions, browser tests will load an entire page and interact with it as a real user does. This scenario could be a checkout page, a form to fill out, or anything you need to verify a page looks and works as designed.

The nature of a browser-based test is to capture a screenshot of any failing pages, providing developers with a live look at what went wrong. These tests are instrumental in guaranteeing the application's stability and give developers confidence in their CI/CD pipeline. This confidence, in turn, creates faster development and deployment time. This time savings is crucial in trying to patch bugs and deploy new features.

I've often seen projects ignore tests in the beginning, during the volatile and quickly changing state. Saying things such as "there's not much to test yet," "there's no time," or "it's not important" can be heard uttered from the mouths of early-stage developers and founders. In fact, this isn't just something that plagues new companies or projects. It happens in large organizations too. Fast forward to your project a year from now, and you'll soon regret not having written these tests ahead of time. Finding the time to test now will pay dividends in the future.

---

[12] Selenium, https://www.selenium.dev

Mix

Mix is a Webpack based asset compilation tool built for Laravel. If you're a full-stack or front-end developer, you'll love Laravel Mix. If you're like me and primarily a back-end developer, you'll grow to appreciate Mix. It simplifies much of the work required to get front-end assets built and ready for production.

Using Mix is entirely optional. If you have a preferred method of handling assets, then perhaps you won't need to worry about this. However, I think even the most novice of developers can quickly harness the power of Mix. Specify the CSS and JavaScript files your application uses, and the output folder, typically `public/css` or `public/js`, and Mix handles the rest for you.

There are several Webpack related features you can make use of in Mix. However, you'll need a firm grasp of how Webpack operates to understand some of the other features. This learning curve shouldn't deter you from using Mix. It's a tool any level developer can and should utilize as it provides your application with immense benefits on the client-side.

A couple of my favorite features of Mix are URL processing and the watch command. Watch will run in the background, looking for any changes to your files. It recompiles the assets automatically for you when it detects them, making your development changes immediately available. On the other hand, URL processing automatically downloads any images referenced in the `url` call, places them within your applications images folder and changes the CSS link to a relative one. That is fantastic for solo developers who can easily forget what they referenced and where. It's also great for deployments. You can reference images hosted on a file server somewhere, such as S3. During deploys, all the images can be downloaded to the local machine. This can significantly reduce the size of your Git repos and deploy bundles.

Chapter

5

Devops Tools

Once your application is ready, how do you share it with the world? You'll need tools that help you manage application environments—primarily production—to ensure your servers and code are running as intended. DevOps tools help us manage server infrastructure using techniques similar to the ones we use for building applications.

This chapter goes over several tools provided by the Laravel that can help you get up and running quickly and effectively. Let's take a look at them.

Forge

We've all been there. A last-minute project, idea, or concept for a VC or client comes in that we need to show off. But, we have nowhere to reliably host it without spending the next several days figuring out how the latest version of NGINX goes with PHP and how those max_workers and memory limits were configured on the last server. Perhaps you have a server running that suddenly stopped working or was compromised by hackers. I had the former happen recently. A server I managed recently started failing to renew its SSL certificates. Therefore all the websites I was hosting were unable to respond to any modern web browser. Of course, the timing of when I found this out was even more inconvenient—during a demo. Arguably I should have had proper monitoring enabled, but that still wouldn't have changed how painful this experience was, more than the experience was trying to fix this server. It had been running for four years without fail, but now I had to figure out my server or build a new one.

Unfortunately, my story is only one of many that I can share. Many of us share this story. Some of us are fortunate enough to turn some of those Vagrant and Docker configurations into Ansible or Chef scripts that can automate server

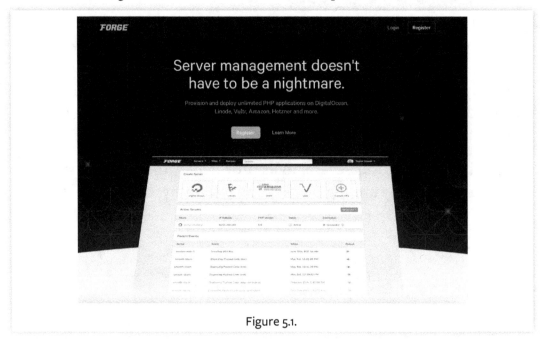

Figure 5.1.

provisioning for us. Many of us, however, are running a side business or working a day job. We can't afford to spend our time re-inventing the wheel. Lucky for us, Forge helps us stay on track with Rule 1 and 2.

Forge[1] is a paid service that handles provisioning and deploying a PHP hosted server for you in one of several cloud host providers, including DigitalOcean, Linode, AWS, Vultr, and Hetzner Cloud. If your provider is not listed, you can go with a custom VPS provider and set up the configuration that way. The best part is that the server is in your cloud host account. Forge does not own it, and you're not locked into the service. Should you choose to stop using Forge one day, your server will continue to run even without a Forge account.

I've used Forge, and it's straightforward and pleasant to use. However, comfort is not a selling point but merely a side effect of a well-written application that solves a pain point many of us share. One important thing to note about Forge is that it is not merely a server provisioning system. It also automatically deploys your applications the moment you push your changes to Git. If you've never used a continuous deployment (CD) system, they are invaluable in providing you with near-instantaneous deployments to production. Usually, you'd have to manually set up this process, which can be quite time-consuming if you've never done it before.

Forge is designed with Laravel in mind. It provisions NGINX, SSL, MySQL, Postgres, MariaDB, Redis, and many more import services. It even supports running multiple PHP versions on the same server, convenient for supporting both new and legacy projects without having separate servers. Part of the challenge in running a Laravel site is keeping the queues running. Forge handles this by running your queues against Redis utilizing a background worker daemon that restarts upon deployment. Using Redis, you're able to take advantage of the Horizon open-source package. We cover that in more detail in the coming chapters.

Setting up a server is one thing. Maintaining it is another. This is why Forge includes automatic database backups to either S3 or DigitalOcean Spaces. Also, Forge handles automatic security updates for your system, so you're always up to date.

There are many things to love about Forge. The online docs describe some of its capabilities best. One way I encourage people to think of Forge is that—on top of

---

[1]   Forge: *https://forge.laravel.com*

everything else—it's a wrapper around what many cloud providers offer but usually requires technical expertise to configure. For example, AWS is a powerful cloud provider that can do virtually anything you need it to. However, if you've ever tried configuring and setting up a network infrastructure with routing and port access, it quickly becomes daunting to set up or make changes to this infrastructure. This scenario is precisely where Forge shines. Managing infrastructure is a full-time job. SRE's, system engineers, these roles exist for a reason because there are many moving parts. Being a business owner and founder forces you to wear many hats. During all the chaos, it's essential for the success of your business and your sanity that you learn Rule 3, "Delegate, even the things you do know." In this case, you can delegate much of the infrastructure work to Forge.

Frequently, we avoid delegating work for cost reasons, which can be valid, especially in a business's very early days. But a fixed price service such as Forge pays dividends for many years to come. Forge currently offers three pricing tiers. If you're just starting, the "Hobby" tier will allow you to provision a single server and deploy as many sites to it as you need for $12/month. Perfect for many beginners who are just trying out a concept. The next plan is the "Growth" plan for $19/month and provisions any number of servers you need. The final one is the "Business" plan, which provides key features a running business will appreciate, such as database backups, automated server monitoring, and sharing your infrastructure with team members, all for the price of $39 per month. One crucial thing to note here, the monthly cost of Forge does not cover the cost of the servers it spins up. Those are billed directly through your cloud host provider as if you had set up through them. The prices mentioned here are for the Forge service only.

For $12/month, you can delegate the hours you'd spend provisioning and updating servers, running queues, configuring security groups, and network routing. You might be like me, and you've run your servers for many years. You've taken pride in it, so surely you'll do it for your own business, right? Wrong. The success of your business is not in who or what sets up the servers. It's in your ability to focus on the primary product you're developing. Your clients won't care if you set up a server that uses 100MB less in disk space than someone else. Even a skilled SRE could easily take 2-3 hours to configure a server from scratch. That's $3–4/hr that you're paying yourself by not using Forge. Hopefully, this is starting to paint a picture that reinforces Rule 2.

Vapor

Having learned about Forge, the next service that we need to explore is Vapor[2]. Forge is concerned with the server aspect of hosting and maintaining a website. Vapor takes this a step further with serverless deployments. Serverless infrastructure isn't actually serverless—there is always a server. In the case of Vapor, the servers are Amazons. Vapor exclusively runs on AWS Lambda. Lambda is Amazon's serverless compute infrastructure with native run times such as Python and NodeJS. However, as is the case with Vapor, it can also run custom container images.

You might be wondering one of two questions. Either you're not a systems person and wondering why you should go with serverless over a traditional server like Forge. Or, you are a systems person and are ecstatic about running an entire application in a serverless environment.

The real power of a serverless infrastructure is in its scalability. The underlying technology of AWS Lambda handles each request independently on a multitude of servers. Given this setup, Lambda allows you to scale up to thousands of requests per second instantly. Likewise, it automatically scales down when there is no traffic,

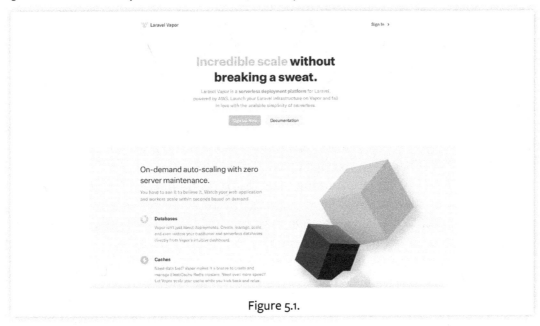

Figure 5.1.

_____

[2]   Vapor: https://vapor.laravel.com

so you only ever pay for what you use. This feature eliminates the need to scale and adjust your servers as demand grows. The second reason to go with a serverless model is that you pay for only what you use. We'll go over the pricing structure in a bit.

Much like Forge, Vapor takes care of all the infrastructure setup. However, given a serverless' distributed nature, it requires running each service for your application outside of the Lambda request. For example, DNS, networking, load balancers, SSL, RDS database, and a CDN distribution with an S3 bucket all get automatically provisioned within AWS for you.

The advantage of such a setup is that you do not have a single point of failure. A separate resource hosts each component of your application. Some resources, such as DynamoDB and SQS, the default cache and queue driver for Vapor, are hosted AWS services. There is no instance to even worry about. Unlike a single Forge server hosting all the required resources on a single server, these resources are distributed and inherently are highly reliable.

You might be wondering about the pricing of Vapor and serverless. Like Forge, Vapor manages the build and deployment of your code, as well as provisioning of resources within AWS. Vapor does not host your AWS account info, and you still must provide your AWS account. You own your AWS resources and are never entirely tied to Vapor. This also means that you are responsible for all AWS charges resulting from using their services. Vapor itself is a fixed price point service of $39 per month or $399 per year.

On the AWS side, however, the pricing isn't as clear. The nice thing about Lambda is that it's pay as you use. If you get zero web requests one day, which is not ideal for a new business but happens, you don't pay anything for web requests that day. One small gotcha here is if you are running many background queues. Vapor handles running those queues within Lambda, and it's beautifully seamless. However, those queues are subject to the same rates. Don't worry, AWS provides a generous free-tier of a million requests per month for Lambda. I encourage you to read their documentation[3] on how Amazon defines a request to Lambda. It's likely not what you think. Many of Amazon's hosted services operate on this type of pricing model: S3, CloudFront, DynamoDB, SQS, and even the serverless version of RDS. Most RDS

---

[3]   documentation: https://docs.aws.amazon.com/lambda/index.html

instances are a fixed instance size, in which case you pay depending on the instance you buy. AWS offers a hosted serverless version of RDS known as Aurora Serverless. It acts much like any other serverless service in that there is no instance for you to manage, no replica to worry about. The database scales automatically depending on your load. If there's no load, you don't pay. Once again, I defer you to Amazon's documentation about pricing as many factors come into play.

While you can only quote me about Vapors' price point, I will share with you an example from a Vapor application I recently deployed. So far, the application is light on direct traffic but makes use of background queues. It makes use of a t3.micro database instance size, and I'm currently paying around $40/mo.

Serverless hosted applications require a paradigm shift in how our applications run. This shift is a transition from our application code running on the same server each time to it running on any server. We no longer can trust that we'll have the same server for each request. In fact, we know we will not. Each request can spin up a new container to handle the load. Then that container might disappear ten minutes later. Any memory and disk storage comes and goes with the container. We cannot run any persistent store in such an environment. Given the ephemeral nature of containers, Vapor is limited to only running the application code within a container. Other services—such as database, caching, uploaded user files—must be stored elsewhere. Vapor ships with a command-line tool that assists in making these migrations. Probably the most significant change a developer has to make is in how resource files are accessed. Upon deploying your application, Vapor packages up all resources in the public folder and uploads them to S3 so that it's hosted behind a cached CloudFront CDN. For Vapor to properly inject the appropriate URLs to the uploaded files within your application, you must use the built-in asset() function within Blade to load these resources. You can no longer get away with just hard coding an image tag like so:

```
<img src="/img/icon.png" />
```

You must do this:

```
<img src="{{ asset('/img/icon.png') }}" />
```

One more gotcha I should warn you about concerns sending emails. Vapor automatically configures Amazon Simple Email Service (SES). However, before you can actually send emails, you must validate your identity within Amazon. Amazon makes a note of this in their documentation. If you've never used SES, it may not be obvious that it's required. Within SES, you can manually specify the allowed recipient one email address at a time, but this is only useful in early development and debugging. To send customers emails, you'll need to verify your identity with Amazon, which can take a day or two.

Serverless isn't for everyone. A variety of services exist to give people options. While every project and developer is unique, serverless and dedicated servers have some general advantages.

Advantages Of Serverless

The first advantage of serverless is something I've already mentioned, which is that it automatically scales. If you have an unpredictable load on your application, serverless may be an ideal setup for you. You might also want to consider going serverless with your database here as well.

The second advantage is that there is no infrastructure to be concerned with. While technically there is infrastructure you should understand, it's not vital. There are no security updates to worry about or a server to rebuild if something crashes. If there is a failure, it'll be on Amazon's side, in which case they're responsible for getting it back up. The disadvantage here is that you have a little less control over your infrastructure stack. While I believe it'll serve many cases, there could be situations where you're better off running a custom solution.

The third advantage I would like to point out is one that can bleed over into the other two, but I think it is worth its own talking point. And that is the fact that with the nature of serverless, you no longer have a vertical stack with a single point of failure. Sure, if any single service fails, your site may become unresponsive. Still, it isolates the specific issue, allowing you to take advantage of potential vendor features such as failovers in RDS. Furthermore, by taking advantage of some of Amazon's hosted services, it reduces the likelihood of a failure. For example, instead of managing a Redis server, pay for the hosted Redis server/cluster for increased uptime and reduced overhead in managing a server.

When To Use A Dedicated Server

On the other hand, if your user base and application load are very consistent day after day, you may benefit from a dedicated server's financial cost savings. With adequate backups, you can recover relatively quickly in the event something does go down. You can also scale it as you need. Amazon offers up to 40% discounts on server and database instances when paying for the year in full. Refer to their online documentation for their current pricing structure.

There could certainly be some scenarios outside of fixed utilization of a server where you would not want to use serverless. One of them that I've seen is if you need your application to have a consistent IP address for network allow list purposes. I've encountered this scenario in government and enterprise network configurations. The nature of serverless does not facilitate a fixed IP address. Along the lines of enterprise, you may be bound by what sort of SaaS applications you're allowed to use. Often with enterprises and government setups, you're forbidden from using outside SaaS applications to access source code or infrastructure. Such situations happen, they're unfortunate, but usually, these environments have dedicated teams for automating deployments and server provisioning within their approved infrastructure environment. This is unlikely to be the case with your side project or business.

What If It's Not Clear Cut

You may have an application that varies in load but not drastically. These situations make it less obvious what the best solution is. I've run into this several times. Make a pro/con list of each setup and go with the one that will meet your needs now or your near-future needs. There's always a trade-off. Just make sure the trade-offs don't violate any of the rules. I find that most of these solutions don't make a massive difference in the financial burden of starting an application, at least not one to prevent you from starting. I suggest just leaving the pricing out of the pros and cons list if possible. That's not always possible, so remember, you're rarely locked into a solution permanently. While migrating infrastructure is painful, it's certainly doable with some forethought.

Envoyer

Up until now, we've discussed a couple of different deployment tools, Forge and Vapor. Both are excellent services that make life much easier. One great feature of these tools is that they not only provision your server's resources but also deploy your code. However, we haven't discussed how code deployments work much up to this point.

In Vapor, due to its serverless nature, your code deployments become zero downtime automatically. Whenever you deploy any new code in a Vapor managed application, your customers see no downtime. Vapor is a special case, and running applications on serverless still a relatively new approach. In a more traditional setup with a VM or physical server, your deployments become more conventional in nature. Instead of simply swapping out the image of the server, you're pulling down the code, compiling/building assets, and running migrations directly on the server running the current code. Typically this causes a downtime where some fraction of users will see a maintenance screen. In Laravel, the `php artisan down` command puts your application into maintenance mode by stopping all writes. When your deployments are complete, you can bring your application back up by running `php artisan up`, and away your application goes.

Sometimes, even a one-minute downtime can lead to business disruptions and impact. If you have a smooth testing and QA process setup for shipping code many times a day, you'll undoubtedly want to ship frequently and during business hours. However, you won't want to interrupt your e-commerce business or delivery driver that relies on your app for instructions every time you have to make a change. You need zero downtime deployments.

This is where Envoyer[4] comes in. Envoyer is a paid Laravel service that connects to any existing server you have and deploys your code with zero downtime. Envoyer does not provision servers. It only connects to existing servers. One additional scenario where Envoyer is helpful is if you're running your application on multiple servers, perhaps it's load-balanced, or you have a queue worker on a separate server. Envoyer deploys to all servers simultaneously with zero downtime. If you already have a server that's provisioned and managed by you or your organization—or you have a Forge managed server—you can use Envoyer to deploy to them while someone or something else manages them.

---

[4]   Envoyer: https://envoyer.io

Envoyer ships with many great features out of the box, such as:

- Native integration with Git hosts
- Heartbeat checks of your applications cron jobs
- Quick rollbacks
- Slack notifications

Plus many more. You can use Envoyer to deploy any PHP project—it doesn't have to be Laravel. If your application has some custom deployment requirements, you can always modify the deployment script as you see fit.

Envoyer is an excellent option for those that need more deployment options than Forge can provide. It's a reliable choice if you simply do not want to violate Rule 2: "Focus on what's important," so you lean into Rule 3: "Delegate, even the things you do know."

Horizon

Laravel has a powerful queue engine, and we briefly touched on this back in Chapter 2. This engine can utilize several back-end driver systems ranging from a database to Redis, Amazon SQS, and Beanstalkd. These queues work by sending and retrieving messages from a queue. However, assessing queue performance is more complicated than one might imagine. If your application is queue intensive, then understanding how these queues are performing is critical for your business. Are any of them failing consistently or from time to time? Is the queue worker running at all? Are there long-running jobs that seem to timeout? Is a batch job partially failing? Has the batch completed at all? How backed up is the queue? How delayed are users' email sends? Are users waiting ten minutes for password reset links? These are all valid questions. This is precisely what Horizon provides.

Horizon is a Composer based open-source package available for anyone to install and monitor their Redis based queues. One thing to be aware of is that other drivers are not supported at this time, although no one says you cannot open a pull request for this yourself. My current project requires using SQS because my project is deployed via Vapor. Vapor currently only supports SQS based queues, even though it supports spinning up a Redis cluster for caching. While Vapor may now be limited to SQS queues, it's possible this could change in the future. In the meantime, Vapor

5. Devops Tools

Figure 5.2.

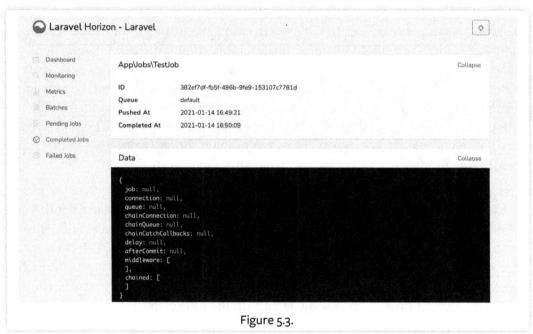

Figure 5.3.

does provide metrics and insights into your SQS powered queues. While not as insightful as Horizon, it can paint a picture of your throughput.

One similarity between Vapor and Horizon is that they are not merely for pretty graphs and information. They also run the queues for you. In the case of Vapor, it sets everything up for you automatically. Horizon does require some setting up, though it's relatively minimal.

Horizon is installed[5] via a few command line calls. After which, it's configured primarily via a single file, config/horizon.php. This file configures queues and workers based on environments. With everything being code-driven, it becomes a breeze to change production level queue code. This file allows you to configure several more important aspects. In particular, you should be aware of the balance options. The balance configuration has three possible values, simple, auto, and false. First, the simple option is the default setting in Horizon and splits your workers evenly across all of your queues. If the email queue and reports queue both have 300 jobs, they evenly share the number of workers available. The next option is auto, which automatically balances your worker queues based on need. If our email queue has 3000 emails queued up and our reports queue has 10, the auto balancer allocates all available workers to the emails queue allowing a few to finish up the reports. Once those finish processing reports jobs, they are assigned to the email queue. With the auto configuration, you can set ranges for the minimum and the maximum number of processes that a queue can consume. The last option is false, which disables balancing queues and falls back to the default Laravel configuration of processing queue tasks in the order in which they're defined in your configuration file.

The Horizon configuration file[6] has more options to play with. The balance option is the most crucial for you to understand as it can directly impact your customers and even your bottom line. Its effects may not be noticeable in a small application running on an underutilized server. However, It can be a drastically different scenario if you are running queues using Laravel default configuration and find yourself with a backlog of unprocessed orders because you have emails being sent to your users.

---

[5]   Horizon is installed: https://laravel.com/docs/8.x/horizon#installation
[6]   Horizon configuration file: https://laravel.com/docs/8.x/horizon#configuration

I've seen these situations happen. I once had a job where we had Laravel's default configuration for queue processing enabled. That worked reasonably well for us as we had a beefy machine. Even as our orders tripled in months, we had no problem kicking up our process count and seeing the server zoom through the jobs. One day, a developer deployed a change to our order processing code. Instead of processing orders for packing on the fly, we were now processing them in bulk batches. During these times of extreme load on the system, no other queues were getting processed. For about 30–45 minutes, no emails were getting sent to customers. Customers could sometimes not log into their account since they could not receive a verification email or password reset email. Even order confirmation emails were delayed during this time. Even worse, some of our internal error reporting emails did not get sent until this queue backlog was cleared. This queue is known as a blocking queue— it blocks all others from doing what they need to do. Nobody intended for this to happen, but sometimes these simple configuration options can make lasting impacts on your business.

This scenario is no different from when I set a large file upload to a server from my home's 5Mb upload link. I thought to myself, "I still have 100Mb download speed. Everything should be fine." It took me a couple of days to figure out why nothing else in the house worked. It didn't dawn on me that even though Netflix was downloading movies, the device still had to make an outbound request to Netflix before it could download anything. This file upload was blocking all other services in the house from performing an outbound request. By throttling my file upload to 2.5Mb, everything else suddenly started working. This is an example of how something small can block everything else, and simple "backoff" implementations or throttling can guarantee you that everything else will continue to run.

This takes me to my next rule, Rule 4, "Pay attention." With so much going on in the world, let alone our side project, it can be easy to miss small but essential details. No one would blame you for not setting the right queue balance option. It's likely the last thing on someone's mind. One important rule about making sure you don't overlook something simple is to pay attention. This doesn't mean you have to know everything about everything, not at all. However, it does mean that if you're choosing to set up Horizon or run your queue worker, take the time to read the documentation in full to understand how it's meant to work. Doing so means taking an additional 5–15 minutes to read and sometimes re-read the documentation to have a good understanding of it. I also feel the urge to rush through and get the dashboard showing as fast as possible. While this might show me a pretty graph, it may not function as intended.

After installing Horizon, it automatically exposes a dashboard at the /horizon URL endpoint. This dashboard is available to you for use in any environment, including production. While accessible to everyone in a local environment, the dashboard is not accessible to anyone in production, only to those in your allow list. You can manually specify which email addresses have access to this dashboard by editing the file app/Providers/HorizonServiceProvider.php. Within that file is an array of email addresses you can hard code. If this list becomes too much for you to hard code, consider querying for the appropriate list of users in your Laravel application and filtering that way. This file is another Laravel gate, so as long as it resolves correctly, you can modify it as you need.

For Horizon to populate its dashboard tables and graphs, you must configure an artisan command that collects metrics to run every five minutes. You can find details about this on the Horizon documentation page[7].

While dashboards are excellent and provide us with useful information, it's rare that we just sit there and watch these dashboards all day. We need to be notified when a queue is not running or is not processing jobs fast enough. We can configure Horizon to send us messages in three possible ways: SMS, email, or Slack notification. Each can also be configured in the service provider file mentioned on the previous page with a single line of configuration.

I've worked with other queue management dashboards, most recently with Sidekiq for Rails. I can confidently say that Horizon is undoubtedly at the top of its class in both quality and data. This is not a knock on Sidekiq, as I think it's a great piece of software. It's instead a testament to Horizon and the quality of the dashboard and metrics that it provides. If you plan on running queues in your application, you should start with Horizon.

---

[7] *Horizon documentation page:* https://laravel.com/docs/8.x/horizon#metrics

Chapter

6

Rapid Application Development

Laravel's ecosystem offers components for managing and developing the front end of an application quicker. Your first decision will be what to build on: Laravel, Spark, or Lumen. Let's look at these three options. We looked at Laravel in a prior chapter, and we won't rehash it here.

Lumen

For some products, mainly if speed or scalability is crucial, you may not need a complete Laravel installation at the start or maybe ever. Lumen[1] is a microframework used for cases where speed, performance, or strict resource considerations are needed. It's ideal for microservices or very lightweight APIs that don't need access to the full framework's features. Lumen achieves this by limiting which of the packages are included in its build. Most of Laravel is built using individual Illuminate packages. Thus, it was possible to slim down the codebase to a minimum by excluding unneeded packages from the Lumen build. According to Taylor Otwell, the actual framework is only a dozen or so files. What's powerful is this: if you begin with a bare Lumen install, you can upgrade to Laravel later on by either including all the necessary dependencies or moving your files over to a Laravel install.

Out of the box, Lumen excludes HTTP sessions, cookies, templating, and more. Other features such as database connectivity, facades, and Dotenv configurations are disabled by default but can be enabled should you need them.

There's been debate as to Lumen's performance compared to Laravel. It very much depends on the operation you're performing. While I'm not interested in starting a debate on speed here, it's safe to assume that Lumen is faster than Laravel. In testing, I've found this to be true as well. However, I've never noticed enough of a gain with Lumen to really justify a need for the reduced functionality. That's not to say that there isn't a need for faster response times. A large-scale API that can reduce response times by even 10% offers significant savings on infrastructure costs—especially when running your own data center.

I've recently started building a small application that will assist me in building an uptime monitor I've been developing. The whole application consists of 20 lines of code, and it's simple but effective. I can scale it with time if I need to. I've been able to write this up using Lumen quickly, and the upside is that it runs a little faster on my Raspberry Pi as a result.

---

[1]   Lumen: https://lumen.laravel.com

Spark

Let's imagine your business idea is a SaaS (Software as a Service) application. For our example, we'll go with an issue tracking application. It's a proven market, and I believe there's room for innovation.

Let's brainstorm some of the features which your application needs that are common to many SaaS applications. First and foremost, our application needs to support users, and those users require a login mechanism. That login mechanism will inherently require a registration form along with password reset options. Next, we need to collect payment from the user somehow, so we'll need to write code that integrates with a payment processor such as Stripe. However, integrating with Stripe isn't as straightforward as merely taking payment. You also have to manage payment plans, subscription billing, cancellations, partial and full refunds, as well as invoices.

However, as our application's popularity grows, we realize that established companies are more likely than individual users to pay for our issue tracking software. However, companies don't want each employee to have to set up their billing individually. So our application needs to support teams and organizations with corporate billing, where administrators of a company can add and remove individuals. Now your application needs to offer a per-seat model of billing. Suddenly this logic becomes quite complicated.

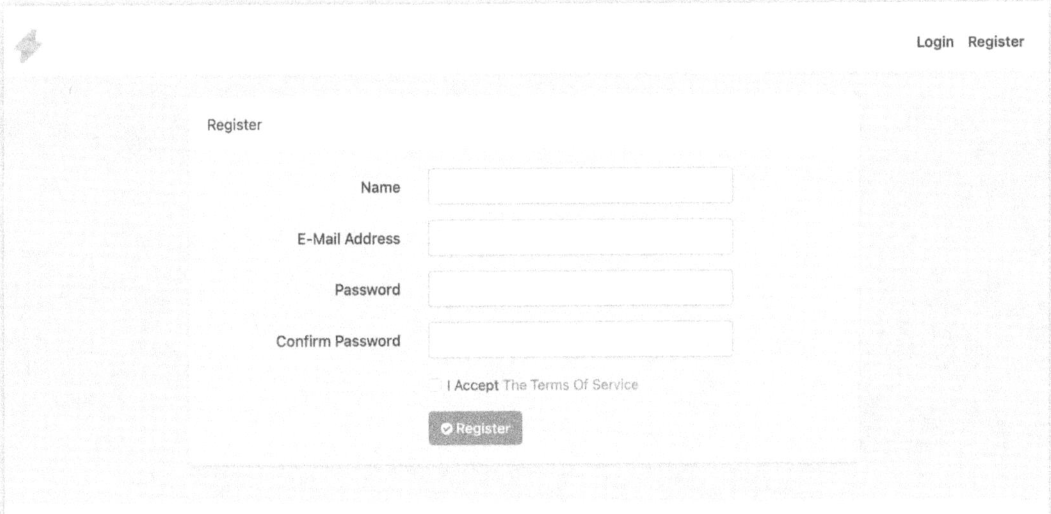

Figure 6.1.

6. Rapid Application Development

A few months go by, and several clients have requested that we allow for programmatic access to their issues via an API. Suddenly we need to extend our application to enable programmatic access. We may not expect to be much of a problem since we created an API for us to use internally. However, clients are not us. They need to be authenticated differently. More importantly, the API needs to be explicitly scoped for them with a token ensuring that they only see their data. Once we release this new API, we want to make sure and announce it to our customers, so they're all aware and upgrade their accounts to our new enterprise pricing plan.

Figure 6.2.

Figure 6.3.

Now that they're on enterprise plans and have their internal systems submitting issues automatically, they need to ensure that all these faulty bugs and internal company dialog stay private. Eventually, they begin asking, "Why don't you have Two Factor Authentication?" So, we rush to implement something that enables it via SMS or email.

We must consider an exhaustive list of features before we even get to how our application does what it does. Have we even picked a name yet? You can quickly get the idea of what you're getting yourself into.

Now, this isn't meant to be a deterrent to starting a project. No one expects an application to start off with all of these features fleshed out. Countless companies have implemented many of these features. Frequently, you can find a good discussion about how to build it, design it, and what approach makes the most sense for your company. But what if I told you there was a better way?

Laravel Spark[2] is a unique implementation of Laravel, which encompasses many of the features a SaaS app may require. All of the features you read that we'd need to offer are already implemented within Spark. Spark has extras that I did not mention, such as avatars on the user's profile, user impersonation for debugging issues, and a dashboard for admins to visualize how well your product is doing. The best part of it all is that it's built on the same Laravel you know and love.

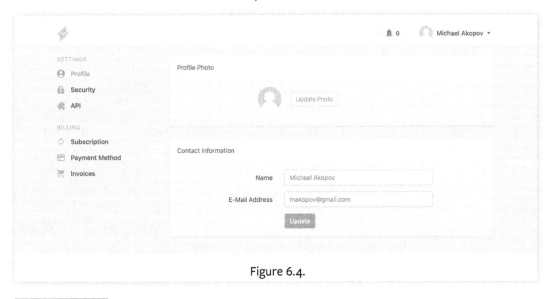

Figure 6.4.

[2] *Laravel Spark: https://spark.laravel.com*

Most of the packages and services I discuss are open-source packages provided by the official Laravel Project. Others, like Spark, are a paid product developed by the creator of Laravel, Taylor Otwell. Spark is not a SaaS app. It's a license-based instance of Laravel. You pay and get a token for use in each project you build. You will receive upgrades for that version of Spark that you bought. One thing to clarify that might confuse newcomers is that Spark's version is not directly tied to a version of Laravel. Instead, a specific version of Spark will give you upgrades of Laravel versions even if that version is a major version jump from 6 to 7.

The pricing is relatively straightforward and a no brainer for everything you receive. As of writing this book, it's $99 for a single site and $299 for an unlimited number of sites per version of Spark. You can upgrade from a single-site license to an unlimited one at a later time. This option is valuable if, later on, you decide you're going to roll out another SaaS app because that entrepreneur fu within you is so strong.

Downsides? The biggest downside is that, at the moment, there is not an efficient way to port an existing application over to Laravel Spark, short of you migrating all of the code into a new codebase. To be honest, I don't see how this could even be done in the future. There is so much that goes into building one that an existing app is likely to have one or more duplicate features already incorporated that require significant rewriting or conflicts. But I hope to be wrong. Perhaps there's a middle ground to be found in the future for existing applications.

Spark is a fabulous and well-written software. However, it is an assumed design model and implementation for your application. While many parts are customizable, you may find that you want to take a completely different approach with one or more of these. That would be completely OK as well.

Spark simply and wonderfully offers a predefined set of resources to launch SaaS applications for many everyday use cases. Spark also facilitates with Rule 2, "Focus on what's important." It's easy to take any of the features I discussed and get lost in the weeds of it, spending days figuring out the best way to do two-factor authentication (2FA) or invoicing. Each and every one of those could be a SaaS of its own. This is why it's crucial to stay focused and focus on what matters. In our example, we're writing an issue tracker. We need to focus on what will make our issue tracker stand out. I can guarantee you it will not be the payment screen or the login screen with 2FA.

Nova

Have you ever wished there was an easy way to build a view for yourself to visualize all those models and all that data you have within your application? If so, then you'll be interested in Laravel Nova. Nova is a paid service from the Laravel team that's designed specifically for building admin dashboards.

Nova takes a configuration-driven approach to specify what fields and models to display data for. It automatically creates a beautiful UI power by Vue.js. The UI supports searching and filtering your data out of the box. And if you have some custom graphs you'd like to display, Nova makes it a breeze to set up custom queries and charts.

Laravel Nova can be installed[3] in two different ways. One is by directly downloading the source code into your application's root directory, and another option is via Composer. After unpacking the source code, you are required to authenticate against your paid Nova account. An invaluable feature of Nova is how it sits in the root of your application directory. While it's separate from the core app, it's possible to get quick updates.

Laravel Nova's pricing is straightforward, much like most of Laravel's ecosystem. You pay a one-time fee of $99 per project for solo developers or $199 per project for teams, including support.

The amount of building blocks you get with Nova is certainly worth the cost. However, Nova may or may not make sense for your project. Since Nova is built as an admin dashboard, the only person you're serving with it is yourself and your team. That's not to say you shouldn't invest in optimizing for your team. If there are tasks you spend a significant portion of your day on and would go faster if you had a UI or some automation for it, go for it! But I would guess that in the early days of being a lone developer, you may not need this feature just yet.

This brings me to rule number 5, "Don't jump ahead." We've all heard the saying, "walk before you can run." A business is no exception to this. While there certainly are moments of making magic happen in any business, you should always think twice about what you're doing and consider if it has real value. Who will this feature serve, and will it help grow the business?

---

[3] installed: https://nova.laravel.com/docs/3.0/installation.html

Figure 6.5

Ultimately you can't forget that the software you're writing is for your customers, not for yourself. It isn't another pet project you can drive to perfection. This is hopefully a company that will outlive you! Dashboards are no different. This advice comes from someone who never thought they'd be saying this because, admittedly, I love pretty dashboards. I always tried finding ways of building dashboards or tools for the developers or maintainers in any project I did, thinking to myself, "if they only gave us time for this" or "if there was only budget enough to build this automation or widget or dashboard." But you're now wearing many hats, and "developer" is just one of those hats. CEO and customer service representative are also your hats. Make sure if you start building a dashboard for your business, you can justify the action, preferably with measurable improvements that the business reap. Sometimes the benefit is obvious, in which case you're thinking I'm just over opinionated on the subject. Other times, you may not be convinced that is necessary.

In Sandy Metz's book *Practical Object-Oriented Design, An Angel Primer Using Ruby*[4], she talks a lot about the subject of premature optimization. In short, she suggests that if you don't have all the requirements for a feature or the future, then don't over complicate it now. Her book is excellent for any developer to read, even if you don't use Ruby. The advice offered can easily apply to any programming language.

---

[4] *Practical Object-Oriented Design, An Angel Primer Using Ruby*: https://sandimetz.com/products

Jetstream

Jetstream[5] is the latest addition to Laravel's frontend scaffolding. With the release of Laravel 8, Jetstream replaced the Laravel UI package. Jetstream takes what Laravel UI offered and builds on top of it with the addition of several frontend components that previously were found only in the paid Laravel Spark version.

Jetstream ships with an out-of-the-box authentication scaffolding much like Laravel UI. The only difference here is the underlying code that powers it. With Jetstream, authentication is powered by Laravel Fortify[6]. Fortify exposes a set of interfaces that streamline developer interactions with user authentication. As per the documentation, it is "interface agnostic." Fortify exposes a set of authentication API's which you can directly integrate with or utilize the scaffolding generated to do so for you.

Figure 6.6.

The latest addition to this is profile management scaffolding. It's a part of nearly any site you build nowadays, whether it's ecommerce, SaaS, or an internal tool for your company. You typically want to allow a user to edit their name, email, or avatar. A scenario many startups don't consider at first is account deletion. To be compliant with GDPR[7] and several state regulations, you must allow a user to delete their account and content (among other things). Handling this is now generated for you with Jetstream.

[5]   Jetstream: https://jetstream.laravel.com/1.x/introduction.html
[6]   Laravel Fortify: https://laravel.com/docs/8.x/fortify
[7]   GDPR: https://en.wikipedia.org/wiki/General_Data_Protection_Regulation

Several other additions include:

- Two-factor authentication, which is crucial today for securing your data.

- API token generation, useful if you will allow programmatic authentication to your website.

- The last one is "teams"—a helpful concept that is now built right into Laravel with JetStream. The amount of tedium it takes to build such a concept into your application can be daunting for early-stage companies. Users can add a team member and they'll be sent an invitation to join your application and the team.

You're not required to use any or all of these features. You can choose which ones your site uses. By default, Jetstreams scaffolding is built with Tailwind CSS for styling and your choice of Laravel Livewire or Inertia for the Javascript framework. They both work exactly the same on the front end.

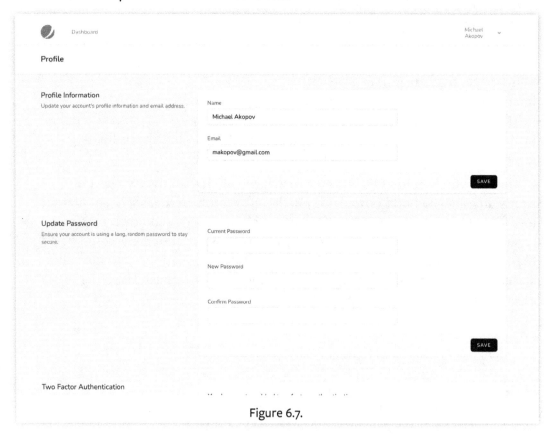

Figure 6.7.

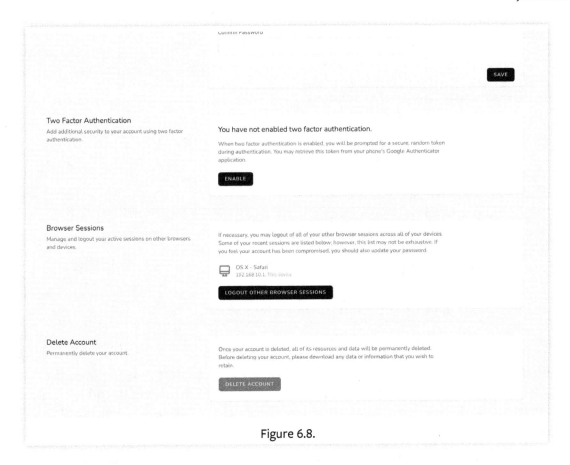

Figure 6.8.

If you're like me, you prefer working in the back end instead of the front end. Whatever your reasoning, if you require any of the features Jetstream implements, utilizing it simplifies your life immensely. This may not always be feasible, depending on where you're at in your development cycle. If you already have a UI for many of these features, this will be irrelevant to you. However, if you're getting ready for a full frontend rewrite or just starting out, give Jetstream a try. Using it is optional, and seeing it in action only takes a few minutes.

Breeze

Jetstream is a feature-rich frontend scaffolding project, which offers many excellent features. However, if you find you do not need robust features such as two-factor authentication or team support, Laravel Breeze[8] may be the right starter package for you to use. It builds a traditional user registration, login, and password reset forms that you would typically expect from Laravel, and it utilizes TailwindCSS[9] to style it. If you prefer to use a different styling framework, you can swap the styling in the scaffolding out with your own.

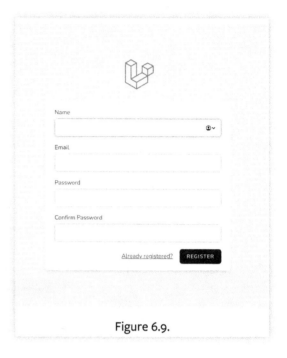

Figure 6.9.

This package may seem very similar to Jetstream, but it differs significantly in the JavaScript used. Breeze comes with little to no JavaScript code to power the Blade forms, making it a vanilla HTML and TailwindCSS setup. On the other hand, Jetstream integrates with a JavaScript framework—either Inertia.js + Vue.js or Blade and Livewire.

It may be confusing to some, especially long time Laravel users used to different scaffolding packages in the past and may be thrown off by how or where to start. In short, if you're looking for a simple starter kit and aren't exactly sure what you need, Breeze is a great place to start. On the other hand, if you're looking for a more feature-rich implementation of front end scaffolding, go with Jetstream. It ships with Tailwind, Livewire, or Vue.JS, all of which are great frameworks. Of course, neither of these frameworks may work for you, or you don't want to take the time to learn them. That's perfectly all right too. You're not required to use either Breeze or Jetstream. You are free to either build your front end code or start with Breeze and then strip out and replace the pieces you do not want.

---

[8]   Laravel Breeze: https://laravel.com/docs/8.x/starter-kits#laravel-breeze
[9]   TailwindCSS: https://tailwindcss.com

I believe some long time Laravel developers were thrown off by the fact that Bootstrap is no longer a supported CSS framework out of the box. They are frustrated by the current state of front end package configurations. While I can understand the frustration with change, it's essential to realize that you're not locked into anything. Laravel is a PHP framework, and it only ever provided UI scaffolding as a convenient starting point. There is no reason to think that Bootstrap—or anything else—won't work with Laravel. There is no shortage of templates out on the internet to drop in and get a functional UI from. Nothing is tying you down to the boilerplate UI. It all interacts with backend API's, and you are free to write front end code that does the same. More importantly, they don't require any changes to existing applications.

I hope this doesn't add any confusion as to where you should start regarding the UI. Many blog posts out on the internet surround this topic, and I encourage you to read through some of them, but most importantly, try these packages out. Start a vanilla Laravel project and play around with Jetstream and Breeze. I did, and I was delightfully surprised by some things!

Figure 6.10.

Chapter

7

Augmenting Laravel

Beyond the tools that the Laravel ecosystem has for streamlining application development, the community around it also shares solutions to frequent problems. Instead of reinventing the same wheels, you should see if someone has released a library that does what you need. This chapter looks at packages to integrate your application with external services and APIs.

Passport

At times your application will need to expose an API for customers to access information programmatically. API designs and implementations vary widely from developer to developer. Each developer's preferences seep through the code into the interfaces of that API sooner or later. However, certain parts of an application must stay consistent from one developer to another for efficiency. As a result, the web community has developed a set of standards that help keep our API's consistent as much as possible from developer to developer. One such standard many are aware of is REST. REST suggests how we should communicate over HTTP with our applications. Another standard revolves around authentication. Authenticating APIs is one of those things that nearly every application needs. However, you rarely want to write on your own due to such an undertaking's inherent complexity and security risks.

This is where Laravel Passport comes in. Passport is an open-source Laravel package that implements full OAuth2 token-based authentication. OAuth[1] is an open internet standard that stands for Open Authorization. Its goal is to provide authentication and authorization to a resource such as a website, all without giving away a person's password. A typical example of this is when you see the "Sign in with Facebook" prompts on certain websites. They use Facebook to identify you, without requiring you to sign up for an account or giving them your Facebook password.

Passport[2] implements OAuth for you and integrates directly with Laravel authentication middleware, making it seamless to give your users programmatic access to the application. It installs like any other Laravel package, via Composer. After installation, Passport generates some local keys. You should never check these keys into source control. You'll instead re-run this command in production.

Passport offers different configuration options to suit just about every need. Much of this can be found on the online documentation and is not worth repeating here. There is one thing I would like to point out, Passport ships with pre-packaged Vue JS components that utilize Bootstrap CSS. These components make it easy to set up a page that enables users to create clients and personal access tokens, removing the need to interact with the Passport internal APIs directly. Of course, if you're not using VueJS, you need to create this UI yourself.

I certainly encourage you to utilize Passport if you're developing APIs. Using Passport enables you to follow Rules 1 and 2.

---

[1] OAuth: _https://en.wikipedia.org/wiki/OAuth_
[2] Passport: _https://laravel.com/docs/8.x/passport#installation_

Sanctum

Authenticating with your application's APIs is something most of us will need to do sooner or later when building a single page application, providing customers access with our API, or simply calling your API using a REST tool. For simple use cases such as these, it can be overkill to install Laravel Passport, especially if you do not have any OAuth 2 requirements.

Laravel Sanctum was built as a lightweight authentication platform for this reason. Many times you don't need OAuth 2 capabilities, so why bother with the setup. Sanctum aims to solve two primary use cases. The first case is authentication for SPA's with your Laravel backend, and the second scenario involves token authentication with your APIs. With this functionality stubbed out, you can even allow users to generate personal access tokens. Sanctum can automatically generate these tokens and authenticate them with no change to how your existing code needs to handle authentication and authorization. You can focus on building the interface for allowing users to create tokens or utilize Laravel Jetstream and let it do it for you.

Sanctum's documentation[3] has excellent information on how to set up your application for SPA, API, and mobile authentication. The SPA setup provides the advantage of its built-in CSRF and XSS protection. They provide JavaScript code examples and demonstrate how to authenticate by passing in a token. They show examples of API tokens, how to generate, revoke, and authorize tokens, as well as neat features like providing them with scopes or abilities like you might see in other access control setups. For example, a user might generate a read-only token, and it's important to mark it as such. Last but not least, those of us who power mobile apps with Laravel can enjoy a bit of fresh air with support for this. You also get specific examples of how to best set up your mobile application to authenticate.

If you need simple token-based authentication, check out the Laravel Sanctum package. This very intuitive gem of a package makes light work of allowing programmatic access to all those API's that you develop.

---

[3] *Sanctum's documentation:* *https://laravel.com/docs/8.x/sanctum*

Socialite

On the subject of OAuth authentication, let's briefly cover Laravel Socialite[4]. It's an open-source Laravel package that integrates your application with many popular OAuth providers such as Facebook, Twitter, Google, and several others. Installing Socialite is as easy as any other Laravel package, via Composer. Once it's ready, your users can log in using credentials from one of these services.

You will need to provide your Laravel application with credentials for your OAuth service authentication. These can be registered on the OAuth provider's portal. For example, to use Google, follow these instructions[5], which outline what you will need and how to create your credentials. Socialite works via two primary methods, typically in a controller. The first is your login route. When your application's front end calls this route, you then call Socialite to redirect the user to the OAuth provider's website for authorization. Once the user authorizes your application with the provider, they are redirected back to your application. This step is where the second method comes in.

The second route you define must be a callback back to your application. Once the provider calls back to your application, you can verify the user received a token and grab any additional user data from the OAuth object and store it locally. For example, your user might have an avatar with Facebook. You can now store this in your database and reference it for their profile.

Socialite's documentation is very straightforward. This is a win for developers as it's quick to set up in your application and provides a low barrier to entry for your users to create an account. This single feature may be one of the most important ones in getting user signups.

You've probably used an application that lets you log in with Google or Facebook—or more recently with Apple. You may notice how convenient it is for a user to create an account and log back in without remembering another new password, much less fill out the form every time. Requiring users to create a new account is a barrier to entry. Believe it or not, the simple notion that they need to create yet another login drives some users away.

---

[4] Socialite: _https://laravel.com/docs/8.x/socialite_
[5] instructions: _https://developers.google.com/identity/sign-in/web/sign-in_

I've had the privilege to work in a couple of industries now where I've been able to observe the conversion rate drastically increase when an individual no longer needs to enter a username and password. I've seen this in several forms: password-less authentication and single sign-on system. Both approaches share one thing in common; the user doesn't need to type or remember a username and password.

By enabling Socialite, you can effectively increase the likelihood of someone signing up for your application by allowing their hands to never leave the mouse. Something like this is a crucial business consideration to make, and I highly encourage you to consider using this gem of a package. Of course, you will still have regular password-based authentication available to your users. Some people do not use social media or prefer to keep the two separate, which merely compliments it with additional authentication abilities.

Cashier

When launching an application, a primary objective after delivering an application as promised is to collect payment. In today's world, collecting payment can be performed many different ways using different providers. Cashier supports the three most popular payment processors: Stripe, Paddle, and Mollie. If you're within the United States, then you're most likely familiar with Stripe.

If your application is a SaaS business model or an e-commerce site with recurring subscription charges, then utilizing Cashier will save you an immense amount of time setting up the necessary API calls to Stripe. Under the hood, Cashier uses an open-source library to make those calls. You could write the calls yourself. However, there is little reason to do this now.

While Cashier may not encompass every feature you need from Stripe or other providers, it does cover most of your needs. If there is a feature that it's missing, you can add this functionality to your codebase using the same underlying Stripe adapter that Cashier uses. For example, when starting a new application, you need to set up your products and plans within the Stripe dashboard. You need to set up the corresponding plans within your application's database. Since it can be a pain to do this by hand, I've added a simple function that does this one-way sync.

I've had to write my own Cashier-like implementations for Stripe in the past. While Stripe has well-organized documentation and solid APIs, it is still a lot of work building out the logic necessary to perform simple operations required by many applications.

Imagine you have a subscription model that offers tiers—say beginner, professional, and business tiers. If a user who's on the beginner plan changes mid-month to a professional one, you need to swap their plans now and prorate them for the month. Cashier makes this a breeze to do with one function call.

Cashiers documentation[6] is extensive, and this book isn't the right place to deep dive into it. Go ahead and review the docs to grasp all of its capabilities and see if it suits your needs. They even provide you with basic UI components for accepting credit card numbers. Letting Stripe handle payments for you is a straightforward way to handle transactions securely.

If your business is not a subscription-based model, you can still utilize Cashier, but the incentive to do so diminishes. You should evaluate your use cases to do the best thing for the business. You will likely want to incorporate other payment methods such as Apple Pay and Google Pay if you're an e-commerce site to make it as easy as possible for people to pay. This is not something that Cashier handles out of the box. However, you may still find it useful for some back end payments and record keeping. I encourage you to explore!

---

[6] *Cashiers documentation:* *https://laravel.com/docs/8.x/billing*

Scout

Many frameworks are missing one crucial feature—search. Luckily for the Laravel community, the open-source package Scout[7] handles this.

There are various ways to implement a search feature. This open-ended aspect of search is what can make it tedious to implement on your own. Over the years, I've worked on several custom implementations for search. Either the framework we used lacked a suitable package, or business rules and contracts restricted us somehow. While search can be tricky, it's almost a certainty in life that your application will need to search for something at some point. Even if you have a great website that's easy to navigate, a significant number of users prefer to just search for what they need in a text box. This feature becomes crucial when your website is difficult to navigate.

Databases are pretty fast these days. In fact, most of what you'll ever need from your application can be loaded quickly from the database with basic optimization techniques like ensuring indexes are used. The same can't be said for search. While you could perform a full-text search on a column within PostgreSQL, this will be quite slow and only bearable for a user if there are only a couple of hundred entries. Beyond that, your users will drop off[8] before the search results ever return.

To return search results promptly, you'll want to utilize something backed by a full-text search engine, such as Elasticsearch[9]. By default, Laravel Scout uses Algolia[10], a third-party SaaS company specializing in providing useful interfaces for creating quick search indexes, similar to how Elasticsearch would. Algolia provides additional software and service features around this.

After many years and iterations of search in various forms, what's amazing is that a single developer can integrate search into their site within the hour. The use cases for this are endless. For example, if you are launching an e-commerce platform, you want to allow a full-text search of your products. To do this, you:

---

[7]   Scout: _https://laravel.com/docs/8.x/scout#introduction_

[8]   users will drop off: _https://thinkwithgoogle.com/marketing-strategies/app-and-mobile/page-load-time-statistics/_

[9]   Elasticsearch: _https://www.elastic.co_

[10] Algolia: _https://www.algolia.com_

1. Turn the `Products` model into a searchable one,
2. Configure the background queue job to index the data, (this is all configuration driven),
3. and then perform the actual search on an eloquent model.

It's quick and aligns with the existing eloquent syntax. For example, to search for "fishing rod", you can do:

```
App\Models::search('fishing rod')->get();
```

Doing so returns a collection of Eloquent models, much like a typical query would.

As with any package, read the documentation for specific implementation details. However, if you're looking to implement search, start with Scout, as it's the most straightforward way to do this. While Algolia is a third-party service, they provide a free tier account to get started. It should allow you to create a proof-of-concept and verify if search works for you on your platform.

Echo

Most modern web applications try to perform client-side requests as much as possible to avoid a full page reload. This practice offers faster render times to keep your users engaged, and it reduces the need to do a full reload just to update a portion of the page. It offers a much nicer user experience that's much more likely to keep users engaged and on the site. This is the case for requests that are simple in nature—perhaps a delete action or a parameter toggle. These data requests are quite simple and can be achieved without a page refresh by issuing an HTTP request to the server and waiting for a reply that can then be confirmed to the user.

This process of issuing requests works well when there is a user-issued action. But some applications—such as data dashboards or even email clients—require real-time data updates. It can be very taxing on both the client machine and server to keep polling for data changes. Doing so can lead to delays in data arrival or over-whelm your server with requests. This is where streaming comes in. By utilizing WebSockets, our browser can listen for any data changes sent by the server in real-time.

Laravel provides us with a package that assists with just that. Echo[11] is an open-source package that seamlessly blends Laravel's backend events with the front-end. This tight coupling of events is a convenient way to maintain consistency. Let's say you have an online food ordering app with separate restaurant and customer-facing dashboards. Once a customer submits a purchase, we raise an `OrderReceived` event on the backend. This event can cause a series of background jobs to run and process the necessary information. Simultaneously, our front end can listen for the same event and automatically update the restaurant's dashboard to reflect that a new order has arrived. Many restaurants are busy establishments. It would be unrealistic for them to press a refresh button every so often to check for new orders. This scenario is where sockets can provide an enormous amount of benefit.

Echo ships with two WebSocket providers out of the box, Pusher and Redis. Both have their unique advantages, but ultimately they both do the same thing. Pusher is a paid service that handles the concern of running a WebSockets server for you. On the other hand, Redis might be preferable if you're running a Redis server for queues or anything else already. The latter would be the most economical setup. However, with Redis, you'll need to run a WebSockets server such as the one from Socket. IO[12]. Doing so is generally pretty straightforward to do. Conveniently, Laravel lets you work with a self-managed or fully managed driver for WebSockets out of the box.

If your application pushes any data near real-time, I highly encourage you to explore using Echo with WebSockets. The performance tradeoffs compared to polling for data over HTTP can be enormous. That's not even counting the modern user experience of a "live" application that a user can experience while on a website.

---

[11] Echo: https://laravel.com/docs/8.x/broadcasting#client-side-installation
[12] Socket.IO: https://socket.io

Chapter

8

Third-Party Support

Until now, we've discussed much of the core Laravel ecosystem—both open and closed source packages and services directly from the Laravel team. These are great packages that serve many of your needs. However, every great ecosystem is made up of its community. The NFL is so vast and impactful due to its large fanbase. Soccer is popular around the world as it also has an enormous fan base. These communities not only sustain but also fuel the growth of these sports. This same sense of camaraderie is true in the software world.

What starts out as a small framework with leading industry changes eventually survives not only on its ability to innovate but also on building a community. Sooner or later, other frameworks will attempt to adopt what made Laravel famous. By that point, though, Laravel will be fueled by its consistent user base. Part of that community includes third party packages, training materials, and software support.

Like before, this chapter dives into some of these third parties and how you might utilize them for your project. The companies outlined below are far from the only ones around. Many are worth writing about and mentioning. I've come up with this list merely from my experience. These companies are established companies within the community. But there are many up-and-coming and lesser-known products, developers, and companies that I encourage you to seek out and support when you have the opportunity to do so.

Laracasts

We've all heard that continuous education is an essential part of life. I couldn't agree with this statement more. It is especially true in business. There is always something new to learn, either about running a business, creating a product, or the technology used in the product.

The most concise screencasts for the working developer.

Figure 8.1.

Even if you already know Laravel, there will always be features you aren't aware of, haven't used, as well there will be new versions of Laravel that you will need to learn. I've personally always enjoyed watching other developers code. There is so much you can learn from other's personal styles and then adapt to what works best for you.

Laracasts[1] is an online subscription course for full-stack Laravel development. The Laracasts website describes it best, "it's like Netflix for your career." Laracasts is run by Jeffrey Way, who does a phenomenal job walking you through step-by-step videos of Laravel—everything from a beginner guide to advanced lessons. Jeffrey's courses are not like the YouTube videos you've seen online. He has a unique ability to make the videos engaging and informative at the same time.

Laracasts offers a wide range of topics, everything from back end frameworks like Laravel, Symfony, and databases, to front end stacks like React, VueJS, Alpine, and Tailwind CSS. Laracasts offers affordable pricing with several different plan options. It is a great way to stay up to date with the latest changes in Laravel.

Laravel News

Keeping up to date with what's going on within the Laravel community is a time-consuming process. There is endless information out there to sift through, many packages, and even more maintainers. Most of us don't have the time to figure out what's going on. My favorite way to stay up to date is with Laravel News[2].

Laravel News is a website and weekly newsletter run by Eric Barnes that provides the community with the latest information about what's going on within the ecosystem. I use it, and I look forward to reading each newsletter every Sunday morning. Laravel News offers a sponsored listings section where companies or individuals can pay to advertise their product or company near the top of the newsletter. Doing so is valuable if you're launching something and want to spread the word about it to a community you're already connected to. While most of us are not very fond of advertisements, the quality of sponsored products shown is high, well-vetted, and, more importantly, applicable to what I might need.

---

[1] Laracasts: https://laracasts.com
[2] Laravel News: https://laravel-news.com

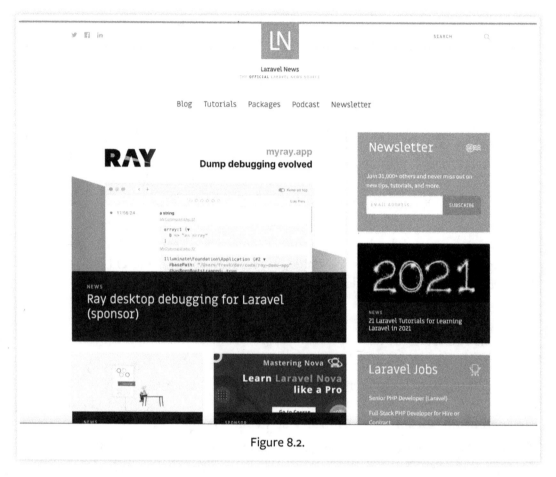

Figure 8.2.

On top of weekly Laravel updates, you also receive links to helpful and insightful articles written by other community members. These are great as they are usually written in the form of a post mortem. They cover issues people experienced with real production applications and how they solved them. On top of that, you get insightful links to software products that exist in the community, along with upcoming event data and even current job postings.

If you're not already a subscriber, go sign up. They'll never spam you, and the consolidation of information is invaluable!

Spatie

When it comes to being an official unofficial package developer for Laravel, Spatie is the gold standard. The team behind Spatie has developed over 200 Laravel packages and has over 75 million downloads combined. Don't take my word for it, in any case. You can find them on Github at https://github.com/spatie and their main website https://spatie.be.

Spatie is a Belgium based web development shop that gained much of its popularity due to their prolific open-source contributions. But Spatie is much more than that. They're a web development shop that can help you build out your entire application if you'd prefer to outsource the work. Spatie also provides many training videos and courses that you can access from their website. These videos are helpful and in-depth discussions of real-world problems and solutions they've encountered while building many of their products.

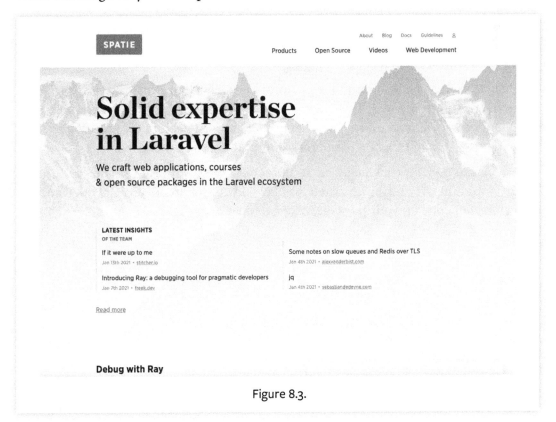

Figure 8.3.

One of their products is Mailcoach[3], a self-hosted email marketing application. It's an excellent alternative to paying for expensive engagement platforms. When you're a small company, spending hundreds of dollars a month on email campaigns isn't possible. You can buy Mailcoach full access for what most companies charge per month—making it a great addition to your email marketing. However, you still need to pay for a mail sending service such as Sendgrid[4] or Mailgun[5].

Another application from Spatie is Flare[6]. Flare is meant to assist you with back end and front end error monitoring and tracking. It's a neat application meant to mimic ignition, the error page of a standard Laravel site.

As I mentioned earlier, Spatie has over 200 Laravel packages. I've used several of these, and they're fantastic for many concepts that probably don't belong in a framework, though many of us utilize them. I use the spatie/laravel-backup[7] library extensively, which is an excellent package for automated backups of your application. You can configure this package to backup automatically with a cron job, and it will backup both the source code and the database. It offers configurable destinations such as the file system, backup directly to Amazon S3, or any file system you have configured within Laravel.

One other package I've found very helpful in nearly all of my applications is spatie/laravel-permission[8]. This package utilizes Laravel gates to allow you to assign roles and permissions to users. This is helpful when you need to give specific users read permission and others write permission to the same set of data.

As you can see, these packages serve a practical and useful role. If you ever find yourself thinking, "I wish this existed," it likely does, and Spatie probably develops it. So before you code up your package, take a look at their GitHub page[9].

[3]   Mailcoach: https://mailcoach.app
[4]   Sendgrid: https://sendgrid.com
[5]   Mailgun: https://www.mailgun.com
[6]   Flare: https://spatie.be/products/flare
[7]   spatie/laravel-backup: https://github.com/spatie/laravel-backup
[8]   spatie/laravel-permission: https://github.com/spatie/laravel-permission
[9]   GitHub page: https://github.com/spatie

Tighten

Tighten[10] is another major player in the Laravel web development ecosystem. Many Laravel web development shops are out there, and while I haven't worked with any of them, many of them have good reputations, and I'm sure they produce great quality work.

However, I still want to call out Tighten. One of the primary partners of the company is Matt Stauffer. Matt is a pillar in the Laravel community. He's spoken at many Laravel events and conferences, and he runs the The Laravel Podcast[11]. Matt does an incredible job of keeping the podcast entertaining, fresh, and always relevant. Both Tighten and Matt run a blog with great material.

If you're considering outsourcing any or all of your developmental needs, Tighten is another excellent choice to assist you and your company in building the product you want. Tighten has worked on many projects for high profile companies.

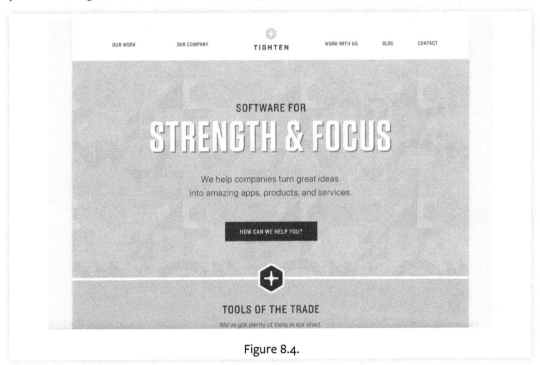

Figure 8.4.

[10] Tighten: https://tighten.co
[11] The Laravel Podcast: https://laravelpodcast.com

Laravel Shift

Eventually, your application will become outdated; new major versions of Laravel are released every six months. You will need to read the upgrade guide and perform a manual upgrade on your application. Laravel does an excellent job of documenting its upgrade guide, making the upgrade straightforward and relatively painless. However, as your application grows, it becomes increasingly more difficult and tedious to perform upgrades. Minor upgrade improvements will undoubtedly slip through the cracks, and this begins to compound quickly if you have more than one codebase to maintain.

Automating Laravel upgrades is precisely what Laravel Shift[12] is built for. For the price of a couple of cups of coffee, Shift can create a pull request (PR) against your Git repository with all of the upgrades made for you. If there's anything it isn't sure about, it skips it and writes comments directly within the PR for manual review.

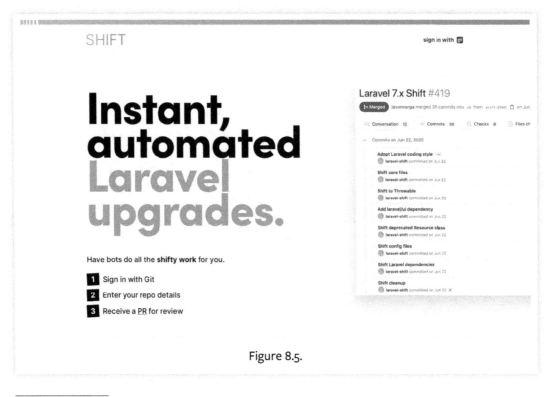

Figure 8.5.

---

[12] Laravel Shift: https://laravelshift.com

Laravel Shift is created and maintained by Jason McCreary, who's done a phenomenal job over the years keeping up with the latest Laravel versions so that upgrades are available right as new versions come out, with little to no delay.

I've used Shift for many of my upgrades, and it has saved me countless hours and headaches of upgrading my application manually. The best part about Shift is that it offers services beyond simply upgrading Laravel versions. Other Shift options include upgrading your Composer dependencies, automatic code formatting, and my personal favorite, Shift writes tests for you. The test generator will create model factories, PHPUnit tests and can even generate browser-based tests—an exceptional value for the price of a lunch.

Shift also offers a few free shifts you can use to consolidate namespaces, move model namespaces, and even lint your code. Shift doesn't just work with Laravel. It'll also run on Lumen, Vanilla PHP, and Bootstrap CSS. That's right. If you decide you want to migrate from Bootstrap to Tailwind CSS, Shift can perform a migration for you.

Shift offers pay-as-you-go pricing. If you have several projects, you can pay for a monthly subscription to Laravel Shift and run it as many times per month as you like. One last note I'd like to make about Shift is they offer access to a private Slack workspace made up of other developers eager to ask and answer questions. This workspace also allows you to ask questions directly to Jason.

At some point, you will find yourself needing to upgrade your Laravel application, whether for feature sets or a security upgrade. You should consider Shift for your next upgrade.

Laravel Debug Bar

When developing your Laravel application locally, you'll frequently find yourself wondering what's actually happening to your site under the hood. Things like "what events are firing, and in what order?" This information, plus much much more, can be gleaned from the Laravel Debug Bar. It's a nifty package every developer should install.

The Laravel Debug Bar is based on the PHP Debug Bar[13]. The Laravel Debug Bar features many add-ons on top of this, which provide Laravel specific details about your application. In addition to what I mentioned above, some of my favorite additions are:

- View insights, so I always know what files load within the context of the current page.

- Queries, which help me understand what queries ran to generate the page.

- Cache, a debug bar that allows you to inspect the cache at the same moment in time.

There are several other very handy features. One other feature is not enabled by default within the Laravel Debug Bar, and that is the Model insights.

After enabling[14] this within your applications debug bar configuration file, you will see a new "Model" tab. This model tab displays all of the models loaded to render this page. This model addition was created by Jonathan Reinink, who provides an excellent course of Eloquent Performance Patterns[15] that you can find on his website. I have found the Models tab to be insightful in tracking down the source of expensive and redundant database calls. In the haste of developing features, sometimes I will forget to check my query optimizations or to eager load some data. Especially when working on personal projects late in the evenings, these things slip through the cracks.

After enabling Models, it's easy to spot pages where all I needed to avoid duplicate queries is to eager load an association or move loading a model outside the scope of a loop. These are simple oversights that can often lead to you loading a User model 20 times on a given page. Over time, these mistakes add up. They slow down your site's responsiveness and can lead to you unnecessarily growing your database resources to keep up with the underperforming or needless queries.

Laravel Debug Bar is a free package that you can install via Composer to your project within minutes. If you are not already using this simple tool, install it first thing after reading this.

---

[13] *PHP Debug Bar:* http://phpdebugbar.com
[14] *enabling:* https://reinink.ca/articles/viewing-model-counts-in-the-laravel-debugbar
[15] *Eloquent Performance Patterns:* https://eloquent-course.reinink.ca

Chapter

9

For Entrepreneurs

Up to this point, we've covered an extensive range of topics, but none of them in-depth. This approach is intentional. The purpose is not to give you detailed information but rather provide a broad overview. We're looking at the forest here, not individual trees. If you didn't know how vast the Laravel ecosystem was before reading this book, you are now well aware and well equipped with the right toolset to tackle your life-changing project.

Going into detail as to what each package does and every little configuration, variation, and combination possible would be time-consuming and impossible to digest in a book. That's why I wrote this book at a high level, with common scenarios used as examples. This book and its examples aim to educate you about what's possible, what answers are available, and under what circumstances. Eventually, you'll encounter a situation or a problem that you may not be aware of how to solve, or you think there should already be a solution. You now have—in the back of your mind—all the various solutions and options we've listed to inform your decisions.

Making Decisions

It's often a challenge to know when to use what package or service. Should I use Vapor or Forge? Should I generate my scaffolding with Vue or React? Should I design my theme or start with a pre-existing one to speed up testing my business idea before sinking too much time or money into the design. These are difficult decisions to make early on in the process. Sometimes, life gives you obvious restrictions that simplify these decisions.

Perhaps you're unemployed and need to start this business with as little money as possible. You may forgo Forge or Vapor entirely and maintain your server. Doing so is both a good learning experience and saves you money. On the other hand, you may be doing this as a side project, after a full day of work or helping the kids with school, which would make the decision to pay a little for even an extra 30 minutes per day of your time back obvious. If you're like me and not good with design work, you'll be happy to find a starter theme to modify rather than trying to design your monstrosity. I love the decisions in life that are obvious. They don't require any adulting!

However, if you've been an adult for even five minutes, you know that life is more often than not a gray area, rather than black and white. You may be like me, a back end developer with sysadmin experience. You've managed your servers before; why not do it now? You can make sure it's done the way you want and save yourself some money in the process. In these situations where you're facing a decision, I find that resorting to the rules helps tip the scales of your decision. When I encountered this same decision, I found that Rule 2 helped me decide to use Vapor to deploy my application. In return for the added upfront cost, I have no servers to worry about, no infrastructure to keep up for my clients, and—most important of all—I can keep focusing on my application.

Surround Yourself

Making decisions alone can be difficult. You'll find yourself in a gray area often. And usually, you will second guess your choices —it might be hours later, or it might be months later. Being the sole founder of a company can be a lonely experience. You'll confront many decisions, highs, lows, bugs, solutions, income, and expenses. You'll experience each of these situations as a founder, sometimes all in the same day. You'll find yourself hitting obstacles, one after another. It can be daunting sometimes. But you must not give up. Each wall you face is merely a stepping stone.

Surround yourself with good friends, regardless if they're developers or not. Help them hold you accountable, motivate you, and inspire you. Find friends that are moving in similar directions, where you can share business ideas and strategies. Even if the businesses are unrelated, it trains your brain to think like a business owner.

Also, find a group of technical people to bounce ideas off of. I say group because you do not want to annoy the same friend many times over. A local meetup is a great place to get feedback on your ideas. But some meetups are enormous and typically not where you're going to get personal feedback. There are plenty of small user groups where you can share your ideas and get rapid feedback. These are also a great way to vet your vision, especially if it's for a technical audience.

Building a Business Idea

Every reader of this book is undoubtedly in a different place with their business. You may have a profitable business already, looking to start number two. In which case, I wish you much success, and I hope that this book provides you with useful insights. Or, this may be your first business endeavor, and you may be wondering where to start. That's an excellent question. It's one many people have asked, pondered, and have opinions. My intention is not to force an opinion of what may or may not succeed. I've come to learn that the right person can sell air to the right people. Everything in life can be negotiated. That said, I'll share the general business ideations that I've seen succeed more often than not over the years.

When searching for your next business idea, you likely have many ideas you've thought of at lunch with friends or over a drink. Most of these ideas are probably not actionable. However, the ones I have seen succeed often do so by solving personal problems and pain points. It's likely that if you're unable to find a product, service, or person that can solve this problem for you, it's unlikely that you're the only one with it.

Other sources of inspiration can come from reinventing the wheel. Believe it or not, many markets have not seen innovation in quite some time. Even if you're serving a niche submarket, you can live a comfortable life if you can obtain 1,000 regularly paying customers. You can directly tap into other markets as an underdog. You'll have some uphill battles to prove yourself. The flip side to this approach is you're no longer proving the market and building a fresh audience. You only need to prove yourself and attract customers.

Some existing markets are either notoriously challenging to get into or saturated with options. If you're bootstrapping the business or it's your first, I suggest you keep it relatively simple. For example, building autonomous vehicle equipment will require large amounts of capital and years of R&D research before you could ever turn a profit. Now, this is an obvious example, but sometimes they're not as apparent. Tapping into the personal task management industry is a common one. Many people have an opinion of what they want from a to-do list. There is little product development involved as the market's well-proven. And technically speaking, it's relatively straightforward to develop. It's a great project to build if you're getting your feet wet. However, the low barrier to entry is equally appealing to everyone else as well. In this scenario, you're likely to discover that the market is full of many options, making it trickier for you to gain a footing.

Budgeting

Most people don't have tens of thousands of dollars to bootstrap a business. Even if you do, I believe you can start a business on the cheap. Once you've decided to start a business, you should set a budget for yourself. Your personal finances will thank you, as will your business. You might be wondering why I say your business will thank you. I've dabbled in many different businesses over the years. Some were mine, and others were not. This experience led me to see some interesting patterns in life. One of them is that money doesn't solve all problems. Sure, it can go a long way, but often you need to limit it. Holding some dollars back can breed creativity.

First-time business owners can quickly justify every little expense, pivot, upgrade, and pay-in-full option they come across. These are usually just noise. By setting a hard budget, you'll be able to check against it whenever you have a financial decision to make. You likely don't need Quickbooks before earning your first dollar or a trademark lawyer on your first week.

With your finances in check, you can start to figure out what you're willing to spend for the entire venture before calling it quits. What's your worst-case exit strategy? $1,000? $50,000? How much are you willing to put into the business before you cut your losses. As much as we all hope for the best, not every business will make it. I hope that yours does. However, it would be imperative to figure out what bottom-line loss you're willing to take.

Goals and Milestones

Strict budgets also lead to goal setting. Goals help you set achievable and tangible tasks. There will be a lot to conquer in the first six months of business, and if you're doing this after the kids go to bed, then you'll appreciate being focused. I have found that the smaller the task is, the more likely you are to tackle it. I often find myself with 20-minute windows where—thanks to my small, bite-size tasks—I can deploy one or two minor improvements.

Context switching is difficult. Find yourself a to-do and note-taking app you're comfortable using. Use them to write broad goals with concrete tasks.

Goals should then trickle up into broader milestones. For example, you may have a first milestone as a private launch of your application in six months. This could be where you allow close friends and family to try out your application. Then, set all the goals you need to achieve to make that happen. For example, they may not need billing enabled or account deletion right away. The next goal could be releasing some major feature that you decided to cut out of the first release, so on and so forth. These milestones may shift or change, and that's to be expected. Your product is young, and a lot will change. You will pivot many times before you find your groove. Often, your customers will drive your innovation and goals. This feedback loop is what you want. The market will be your greatest product roadmap. Until you're at that point, clear, concise, and measurable tasks, goals and milestones, help you get there.

Promoting and Marketing

All of your hard work would go to waste if you cannot get anyone to use your application. Receiving your first clients may be the most challenging aspect of your project. Promoting your work can feel dirty to most developers. We're not used to the spotlight, the fancy words, hook-lines, one-liners, and charismatic charm that it takes to convince people they should buy your product.

However, marketing your products doesn't need to feel sleazy. There are many good examples out there of people who promote their products without mimicking the stereotypical used car salesman strategy. In fact, all of the third-party providers I wrote about do a great job of marketing without pushing sales. They provide quality products for fair prices.

It also comes down to your target audience. All of the third-party providers I mentioned target developers as their customers. Developers tend to not do well with sleazy sales tactics, and they tend not to like paying for things. However, it's possible to strike a harmonious balance of quality, value, and fair pricing. However, what if your customer audience is broader? Say you're selling outdoor camping gear. Your audience will be very wide. In which case, as much as I hate to say this, you may benefit from well-placed ads on social networking platforms and other channels. I am careful about this. I do not like ads. However, I've seen how much they can drive revenue to companies.

Running ads can quickly burn a hole in your pocket. While there are use cases for them, I would advise you to take different approaches, especially early on. Many developers spend years posting free content about their journey to building a product. Over time, they grow a target audience, and when they do finally launch something, they have a foundation of followers who will sign up. Doing so is a very time-consuming process, but it can pay off immensely if you take the time and energy to build a quality following.

When to Launch

An important part of creating a product is knowing when to launch. You've often heard the phrase "timing is everything," timing the release of your product is equally important. There are undoubtedly many considerations to make when launching something. Many thoughts run through your head:

- "is it good enough?"
- "will anyone pay for it?"
- "my competitor has 30 more features than I do."

Write all these thoughts down on paper and then throw them away because they're about as useful as any other trash. You already know that not everyone will sign up for your product, but some will. Those who don't might nudge you to correct course with your product and then join when you rework that feature.

This is both a crucial point and Rule 6, "Let your customers drive your feature set." Do not assume you alone know what your customers will want or will have it correct at the start. Focus on developing the core offering of your application, don't get sidetracked with nice-to-haves. Exporting to Excel from your budgeting app is not crucial, it's a nice-to-have. You're assuming most of your clients are looking to jump back into Excel. Maybe they're trying to get away from it and your product is what they're looking for? With that in mind, you'll want to launch as early as possible and get feedback as quickly as possible to get new feature development underway soon as you can. Iterating based on real feedback beats trying to have it all (and guessing wrong) when you launch.

If you're like me, you'll never think your product is good enough to launch—and maybe you're right. If it's not mature at its core offering, it is best to wait and polish the details and review quality control. Make sure your documents are well written for beginners to use. Give some friends beta access to give you critical and honest feedback.

I've heard the saying before, and I'll repeat it here, instead of creating the MVP (Minimal Viable Product), create an MLP (Minimum Lovable Product). Meaning, create just the core focus of your application, make it well and usable, then launch. Don't add anything extra. I read that when Basecamp[1] launched, they had no way

---

[1]   Basecamp: https://basecamp.com

to bill users. This situation was fine since users automatically received a 30-day free trial, so developers had 30 days to add the billing feature. It's amazing what you can do without. You'll be surprised by how willing people are to try non-mainstream products.

In short, create a minimum lovable core product feature and get it out the door. Sign some users up, onboard them personally, collect feedback, iterate on the code, repeat. The faster users get the features they want, the more likely they are to stay and promote your product.

Conclusion

Ultimately by starting a business, you've chosen to set a new path—to create something that no one else has before. It'll take your time, energy, and money to do so. The best way to guarantee neither of those things goes to waste is by having a plan, sticking to it, and evolving that plan as you grow. You won't be the same person or business in a year, so neither should your plan. However, it is vital that you have one so you're not aimlessly drifting around. It's the perfect time to grab a notebook or a whiteboard and layout what your vision, goals, financial constraints, and time-lines look like. Be honest with yourself, then sleep on it, and sleep on it some more. Then revisit it. It's OK if this takes you some time to come up with. Life is a marathon. Unless you're in a particular time crunch to launch something, it's likely that your business can spare a week or two of vision and goal setting.

Chapter

10

For Enterprise

Over the years, I've repeatedly heard about how PHP and especially Laravel are not suited for "Enterprise." These were discussions I've seen take place in person at company meetings, on Twitter, Reddit, and many other forums. In order to understand this bias, we must first understand PHP's background.

PHP's Roots

Without going into too many specifics, let me run you through the elevator history lesson. In 1994, the initial version of PHP came out. These early versions of the language were actually not an attempt to create a programming language. It was merely a way to build dynamic websites, exactly what Rasmus Lerdorf did when creating PHP. He was only trying to build his Personal Home Page (PHP). PHP evolved rapidly over the years. Its low barrier to entry, familiar syntax, and web-specific capabilities made it quickly a favorite for many developers to use.

This high adoption rate led PHP to run much of the web. PHP evolved for many years as a language without any formal specification. Many developers reinvented the wheel with every project, leading to much confusion and frustration within the community whenever someone had to maintain a new project. Over the years, newer options for websites came out, such as Ruby on Rails, Django, NodeJS, and many more. People quickly adopted these new languages, which solved many of the frustrations PHP left developers with. They had a formal specification and were built for the modern website. They were faster and easier to use. More importantly, they were based on a set of standards. Standards make projects predictable, consistent, and reusable. This—along with other things—led to the quick adoption of the notion that PHP is not suited for enterprise applications.

Honestly, there was a lot of truth to the statements. PHP as a language had fallen behind the times and become too comfortable. However, it has since made up for that[1]. But there was one particular bias from those jumping ships that I found to be incorrect. They often compared PHP the language to other frameworks, say Rails. It is a faulty comparison. PHP can only be and should only be compared to the Ruby language. You'd then have to compare Rails to the PHP equivalent at the time, which did not exist. Sure, there were attempts made, but nothing stuck, until Laravel.

---

[1] *it has since made up for that: https://php.watch/versions/8.0*

Enterprise Needs

Enterprises, or any company large enough to have departments of developers, are looking for consistency and formal specifications that the individual departments can abide by to reduce common interdepartmental frictions. Now, this is an oversimplification of how company dynamics may work. Each place is drastically different. However, I believe this to be the basis of many businesses looking for an "enterprise" ready language.

Java became synonymous with "enterprise." The Java language is backed by Oracle and provides contracts and specifications for nearly everything the language can do. It has an opinionated way of how you should be writing your code, making code quality tracking easy for management to interpret. When every developer knows the details of Java's best practices, managers can move developers across departments with little overhead to learning a new stack.

Fast-forward to today. You find many people who still hold a bitter view of PHP—with its lack of standards and formal specifications. PHP has changed drastically since 2014 when its first formal specification was announced. Since then, PHP has introduced numerous features that other languages offer and improved performance by leaps and bounds. Unfortunately, many PHP websites out there are still running older versions of PHP that are no longer supported.

That is a high-level overview of where the majority of negative opinions about PHP came from. I'm sure many of you reading this will have different opinions, experiences, and stories to share about this topic. Feel free to write them to me. Maybe they'll become the topic of another book! I certainly have felt many of these pains myself and have used other languages, drifting in and out of PHP projects throughout the years. In some sense, it's because of drifting between projects that I've concluded why many people dislike PHP. In fact, most people I talk to about PHP are surprised that PHP is still a language or that developers still create projects with them. Most had a bad experience in the early to mid-2000s and left the community, never to look back. It's hard to blame them for it. They needed something modern, forward-looking, and consistent.

I've migrated many existing 5.x PHP projects into 7, and it continually reminds me why PHP became frustrating. And then I work on a modern project using Laravel—though most modern PHP frameworks share similar concepts, think Symfony—and it's a night and day difference.

These days, I write Laravel and Ruby on Rails code, and seeing the similarities between the two frameworks is very intriguing. Each framework approaches the same concepts and challenges slightly differently. Whether there's a language constraint involved in that decision or something else is part of the fun in comparing the frameworks. With this side-by-side work of both frameworks, I can see why many companies enjoy using Ruby on Rails. After all, it powers some of the most widely used websites out there: GitHub, Shopify, Twitter, Hulu, Basecamp, and many others. Yet, I also see many of those same traits and offerings from Laravel. When comparing PHP—and to a lesser extent Laravel—to other languages, the gap of not being enterprise-friendly has shrunk to near indistinguishable differences.

Another enterprise-friendly concern that companies typically express is commercial support. It's often joked that if you're taking your SaaS company from professional services to enterprise-ready, then all you need to do is raise prices drastically and offer live technical support. In reality, this isn't too far off the mark. Sure, there are some compliance, SLA, and data retention considerations you want to make for enterprise applications. However, most of the time, companies are looking for that support. Organizations have many developers with different needs, providing that 1-1 time can drastically improve their experience and likelihood of retaining your services.

RedHat built a billion-dollar business around this. They offered essentially everything that CentOS does, but with paid support. Now, among other things, that paid support comes with additional features for security patching of packages that are no longer maintained, as well as other offerings, but the core business is a support model.

Laravel's Suitability

Laravel is no exclusion to this list, however. Many companies offer professional Laravel services to large Fortune 500 companies, and the Laravel website showcases a list of its direct partners. These are reputable software companies based all around the world that can be hired by your enterprise to assist in projects, migrations, upgrades, planning and architecting, or anything else you need with Laravel.

There is no reason you cannot use Laravel for enterprise-level work. If you're working for an enterprise and considering using it for work, there are many considerations you need to make. If your enterprise doesn't already use PHP in any capacity, then it honestly doesn't make sense to introduce a new language that no one will be familiar with. However, if you're flexible in choosing a language or framework, then I'm glad you're reading this. Feel free to reference this book and the information I've outlined to support your case for using Laravel. You can tailor your pitch for the sorts of things companies look for in a framework selection.

One consideration you'll need to make in your pitch is how well the framework integrates with existing systems. Will it work with Active Directory or Okta? Can it log to our centralized logging system? Can we audit the code, perform security reviews, receive critical vulnerability alerts, or run a secure PHP system? The answer to all of those questions is yes. I've used Laravel for an organization of over 4,000 to integrate with Active Directory and provide native single sign-on using a community package. By utilizing monolog, I could conform to our centralized logging needs for auditing and debugging purposes. In that same environment, we were deploying applications via container services. So, merely packaging up the entire application into a Docker image was no different from deploying any other application.

If you're already working in an enterprise that utilizes Laravel, then you do not need to convince management of Laravel! Congratulations! Perhaps your company is looking at how it can take its Laravel experience to the next level. Maybe you're struggling at hiring quality engineers or getting access to quality training materials. If that's you, then the products and services covered in previous chapters are an excellent starting point for you.

Chapter

11

Closing Remarks

At this point, you've read about the entire Laravel ecosystem, free packages, and paid services by both Laravel and the community. I've shared insights, thoughts, and suggestions about starting a business with Laravel. Much of what this book covers only scratches the surface—this book aims to cover the community's broad spectrum. Taking the plunge on a framework and ecosystem upon which to build a business is risky. It's essential to look at all of the macro factors along with specific micro ones, such as any specific or unique integration requirements that you might need to consider.

If you're a new entrepreneur, you'll find and value the support that this community provides for early entrepreneurs. The Laravel company itself is a small one building software products. They are building free and paid services and packages precisely for you.

You've seen me reference my six rules for starting a new business project. These rules have helped clear up some uncertain choices I had to make along the way. It can be a lonely road at times, and you'll need some help making a decision. These rules can assist you too. We've all heard the saying that rules are meant to be broken. I couldn't agree with that more. These rules, like most, are intended to be guidelines. The software world is full of these rules. However, no rule-maker could ever predict every scenario. You should do what makes sense, and don't make sense of what you do. Use the rules, adjust them as needed.

There are many decisions to make when choosing a framework that the entire organization will build upon—be it a new company or 10,000 employee enterprise. It can be a stressful decision to make that often comes down to non-technical considerations. This book can help you find the answers you need. I'm always intrigued by the light bulb moments people have, the tipping point in the decision. If this book helped you make a decision, or if you're still on the fence about the decision, please reach out. I'd be happy to brainstorm with you to help you make the best decision for you.

Happy coding, and best of luck.

Chapter

12

The Rules

Rule 1: Go with what you know

You'll have many firsts and new things to learn with starting a business; reduce the unknowns as much as possible during this process.

Rule 2: Focus on what's important

Don't get sidetracked with things you *can* do, instead focus on the things you *should* be doing.

Rule 3: Delegate, even the things you do know

Find ways to free yourself up to focus on what's important, pay for a service to do something you're doing, hire someone, enlist your spouse, whatever it takes to focus on your core product.

Rule 4: Pay attention

It seems like all entrepreneurs have ADD. This statement isn't a medical diagnosis but rather a symptom of the inherent culture of busyness. With so much going on, it's easy to want to rush through what you're doing. Don't let important details slip through the cracks.

Rule 5: Don't jump ahead

We all have dreams and aspirations for ourselves and our businesses. However, it's important to realize where you're at and not try making your business run before it can crawl. You probably don't need that 8TB NAS right now—a thumb drive will suffice. You probably don't need to pay 3k on marketing ads when a few blog posts can get you enough users to keep you busy for a while.

Rule 6: Let your customers drive your feature set

Don't overcomplicate early-stage development and product building, and certainly don't assume you know what your customers will want. Focus on the core product, make that good, then let your customers tell you what they want.

A. Recommended Readings

The following is a list of books that I've found particularly helpful and worth reading. They are in no way endorsing me or this book, rather a personal suggestion of mine. No single book was better than another, each taught me something valuable, and each had something I disagreed with, but they were all worth reading.

- *It Doesn't Have To Be Crazy at Work*
  by Jason Fried and David Heinemeier Hansson

  An excellent read on how to run a company that people will want to work at, cut out the noise and focus on what matters. Fantastic read, even if you're working for someone else. It helps you know what healthy things to expect from an employer.

- *Getting Real: The Smarter, Faster, Easier Way to Build a Successful Web Application*
  by 37Signals

  This book is excellent at getting down to what matters when building a product. It expands on many things I've touched on in this book.

- *The Pragmatic Programmer*
  by David Thomas and Andrew Hunt

  This is an excellent book on how to design technical implementations in your code better.

- *Practical Object-Oriented Design: An Agile Primer Using Ruby*
  by Sandi Metz

  Primarily a Ruby book but all of the practices are applicable elsewhere. It's a good book on how to design object-oriented applications that properly describe and test what you're building.

A. Recommended Readings

- *The Lean Startup*
  by Eric Ries

  Provides a good read on how to start a business and run it effectively, with some great out of the box advice and thinking.

- *Rich Dad Poor Dad*
  by Robert T. Kiyosaki

  This book covers many wide-ranging financial tops but primarily deals with a shift in mentality from working for money to building something that will earn you money.

- *Rich Dad's Guide to Investing: What the Rich Invest in, That the Poor and the Middle Class Do Not!* By Robert T. Kiyosaki

  This book builds on *Rich Dad Poor Dad* but focuses more on the investment side of things. While not directly about building a software business, it helps expand your horizon a bit if you're new to business and investing.

Index

php[architect] Books

The php[architect] series of books cover topics relevant to modern PHP programming. We offer our books in both print and digital formats. Print copy price includes free shipping to the US. Books sold digitally are available to you DRM-free in PDF, ePub, or Mobi formats for viewing on any device that supports these.

To view the complete selection of books and order a copy of your own, please visit: http://phparch.com/books/.

- **PHP Development with Windows Subsystem for Linux (WSL)**
  By Joe Ferguson
  ISBN: 978-1940111902

- **WordPress Development in Depth**
  By Peter MacIntyre, Savio Resende
  ISBN: 978-1940111834

- **The Grumpy Programmer's Guide To Testing PHP Applications (print edition)**
  By Chris Hartjes
  ISBN: 978-1940111797

- **The Fizz Buzz Fix:**
  Secrets to Thinking Like an Experienced Software Developer
  By Edward Barnard
  ISBN: 978-1940111759

- **The Dev Lead Trenches: Lessons for Managing Developers**
  By Chris Tankersley
  ISBN: 978-1940111711

- **Web Scraping with PHP, 2nd Edition**
  By Matthew Turland
  ISBN: 978-1940111674

- **Security Principles for PHP Applications**
  By Eric Mann
  ISBN: 978-1940111612

- **Docker for Developers, 2nd Edition**
  By Chris Tankersley
  ISBN: 978-1940111568 (Print edition)

- **What's Next? Professional Development Advice**
  Edited by Oscar Merida
  ISBN: 978-1940111513

- **Functional Programing in PHP, 2nd Edition**
  By: Simon Holywell
  ISBN: 978-1940111469

- **Web Security 2016**
  Edited by Oscar Merida
  ISBN: 978-1940111414

- **Integrating Web Services
  with OAuth and PHP**
  By Matthew Frost
  ISBN: 978-1940111261

- **Zend Framework 1 to 2
  Migration Guide**
  By Bart McLeod
  ISBN: 978-1940111216

- **XML Parsing with PHP**
  By John M. Stokes
  ISBN: 978-1940111162

- **Zend PHP 5 Certification
  Study Guide, Third Edition**
  By Davey Shafik with Ben Ramsey
  ISBN: 978-1940111100

- **Mastering the SPL Library**
  By Joshua Thijssen
  ISBN: 978-1940111001

Feedback and Updates

Please let us know what you thought of this book! What did you enjoy? What was confusing or could have been improved? Did you find errata? Any feedback and thoughts you have regarding this book will help us improve a future edition.

From the Publisher

To keep in touch and be notified about future editions to this book, visit http://phparch.com and sign up for our (low-volume) mailing list.

You can also follow us on twitter, @phparch, as well as on facebook: https://facebook.com/phparch/